Competition and Credit Control

To my wife

Competition
and Credit Control

K. K. F. ZAWADZKI

BASIL BLACKWELL · OXFORD

First published 1981
Basil Blackwell Publisher
108 Cowley Road
Oxford OX4 1JF
England

British Library Cataloguing in Publication Data

Zawadzki, Krzysztof Konrad Feliks
Competition and credit control.
1. Banks and banking – Great Britain – History
I. Title
332.1′0941 HG2994

ISBN 0-631-12724-0
ISBN 0-631-12545-0 Pbk

Printed and bound in Great Britain at
The Camelot Press Ltd, Southampton

Contents

Preface

The book is a study in depth of the structure and working of the competition and credit control system. This system was introduced in September 1971 with two main aims: to establish a framework within which banks, finance houses and some other financial institutions could operate freely, competitively and efficiently; and to enable the monetary authorities to exercise broad but firm control of the total magnitude of the principal activities of these institutions.

I have written this book primarily for undergraduates whose courses include the study of money and banking; my aim has been to provide them with information on and an analysis of the working of the UK monetary system, particularly of its responses and adjustments to monetary policy measures taken by the authorities.

The book opens with an examination of the structural and operational characteristics of the UK banking system in the middle and late 1970s (chapter 1), and this is followed by a discussion of the reasons for and of the effects of the now widespread practice of liability management – or interbank competition for deposits (chapter 2). These two chapters present the background, some familiarity with which is needed to understand the reactions and responses of banks and other institutions to pressures generated by official action. Chapter 3 contains a detailed description of the competition and credit control scheme as originally introduced and of subsequent amendments and reforms. The problem of the supply of reserve assets to the banks is the subject matter of the next two chapters; more specifically, the possibility of the creation of reserves by independent operations of the banks and discount houses and the relationship between public sector borrowing from the banking sector and the flow of reserve assets to the banks are examined in depth in chapters 4 and 5 respectively. The adjustment process set off by an initial action taken by the monetary authorities, e.g., a call for special deposits, and leading to a change in the stock of money or in the rate of growth of the stock of money is analysed in detail in chapter 6, special attention being paid to the role of interest rates. While the course of the adjustment process is examined in considerable detail, in order to make exposition clear and succinct I virtually left out of account the bearing on various reactions and responses of the uncertainty necessarily surrounding investment decisions, of the general climate of expectations, of changes in expectations, etc. Chapter 7 is a survey of the monetary effects produced by (ordinary) special deposits between 1972 and 1978, and chapter 8 contains an examination of the nature, working and effects of the instrument of supplementary special deposits ('the corset'). Finally, chapter 9 is devoted to an extensive discussion of the general nature of the competition and credit control system and of its principal specific characteristics.

After the book had been completed, the Bank of England and the Treasury issued their Green Paper on monetary control. A Postscript has therefore been added to the book to offer a few comments on the authorities' views on problems of monetary control and on their proposals – set out in the concluding chapter of the Green Paper – for the reform of the competition and credit control system.

It is a pleasant duty to express thanks to my colleagues in the Department of Economics, University of Newcastle upon Tyne, for their helpful comments, particularly to Dr I. Weir, who read the whole book in draft and made several valuable suggestions. My thanks are also due to Mr C. H. Lam for his help in the processing of statistical data. Needless to say, the responsibility for the views expressed in the book is entirely mine.

Department of Economics K. K. F. Z.
University of Newcastle upon Tyne

CHAPTER ONE

Banks and Financial Markets

Banks Operating in the UK

Apart from the Bank of England, which, as the central bank, occupies a very special position in the system, there are now nine groups of banks[1] operating in the United Kingdom:

London clearing banks
Scottish clearing banks
Northern Ireland banks
accepting houses
other British banks
American banks
Japanese banks
other overseas banks
consortium banks

It must be noted that the above classification is based on the characteristics of the formal status of banks rather than on the principal features of their operations in the UK. Because of this banks placed in a particular group are in many cases very different from one another (e.g., the group of other British banks includes merchant banks like Henry Ansbacher & Co., Johnson Matthey Bankers Ltd, etc., side by side with the Co-operative Bank and Yorkshire Bank Ltd, which operate, on a limited scale, like the clearing banks).[2] On the other hand, the nature of business and the methods used by accepting houses, other British banks and many overseas banks are in many respects very similar. Revell[3] suggested that the basic distinction was between deposit banks (including London and Scottish clearing banks, Northern Ireland banks and a few small deposit banks now placed in the other British banks group) and secondary banks (comprising accepting houses, other British banks, overseas banks and consortium banks).

In the second half of the 1960s Professor Revell's distinction between deposit banks (for most purposes, in effect, London and Scottish clearing banks)[4] on the one hand and secondary banks on the other was very significant and useful. Banks in the two major categories were in many respects fundamentally different in character and therefore operated in different banking fields with only a limited overlap and very little direct competition.[5] Moreover, methods and practices of secondary banks were different from those of deposit banks and so were, consequently, their reactions to external pressures and stimuli. Finally, secondary banks were outside the ambit of official monetary controls, though lending ceilings were extended to them when their importance as lenders increased.

During the 1970s, partly because of the trends in the development of the banking system and partly owing to the nature of the competition and credit control system introduced in 1971 and to its applicability to all banks, the differences between clearing and secondary banks have greatly decreased. Clearing banks have developed several classes of business which previously they had been content to leave almost entirely to secondary banks. In order to compete successfully in these new fields they found it necessary to alter their methods, in many cases adopting those employed by secondary banks. Although the business of clearing banks remains significantly different from that of other groups of banks, most of the differences can now be regarded as ones of degree rather than of kind. Some of the differences (and similarities) in the structure of sterling business[6] of the various groups of banks are clearly apparent in the data presented in tables 1 and 2. These tables show the structure of sterling deposits and assets respectively in terms of average ratios for the periods[7] May 1975–December 1977 and January 1978–October 1979 – the middle and the late 1970s. Standard deviations are in most cases low and some are very low, indicating that the arrays of averages give a true picture of the structure of the banks' business and also that, in the second half of the 1970s, while the total volume of the banks' business in sterling increased very substantially its structure remained remarkably stable.

Table 1 shows clearly that the business of the two groups of clearing banks and of Northern Ireland banks is predominantly in sterling whereas accepting houses and other British banks carry out about half their business in foreign currency, and that overseas and consortium banks operate mainly in foreign currencies. There are three obvious reasons for this feature of the system:

(1) The traditional concentration of the clearing and Northern Ireland banks was on domestic sterling business – before 1971 they did very little business in foreign currencies;
(2) many foreign banks established London offices specifically for the purpose of taking part in the lucrative Eurocurrency business;
(3) accepting houses, other British banks, overseas and consortium banks engage in many classes of international banking business, much of it, naturally, in foreign currencies.

The proportion of sight deposits is considerably higher for the clearing and Northern Ireland banks than for the others.[8] This reflects two things: (1) the clearing and Northern Ireland banks are the main operators of the mechanism of payments; they perform this function by transferring sight deposits of payers to the accounts of payees – deposits held with a view to making payments tend to be held with clearing rather than other banks; (2) before 1971 clearing banks took only one class of time deposits – at seven days' notice – at a uniform, low rate of interest, and thus they allowed other banks to capture the market for longer (usually fixed)-term deposits at interest rates comparable to those obtainable on money market assets of similar maturities.

London and Scottish clearing banks obtain over 80 per cent of sterling deposits from UK non-bank customers; deposits placed by other banks and issues of sterling certificates of deposit (CDs)[9] constitute a comparatively minor source of sterling deposits for them. All other groups of banks obtain substantial proportions of sterling deposits by taking funds from other banks and by issuing sterling CDs. Overseas customers constitute an important source of sterling deposits for other overseas banks – this reflects the fact that this group includes several banks concerned with the financing of trade, still largely conducted in sterling, between the UK and the Commonwealth and ex-Commonwealth countries. Until the end of 1978 overseas customers provided a quarter of sterling deposits of Northern Ireland banks. This

TABLE 1 *Structure of Sterling Deposits of Banks in the UK*

	Share of total sterling deposits of the banking system (%)		Total sterling deposits as % of total sterling *and* foreign currency deposits		Sterling *sight* deposits as % of total sterling deposits	
	Mean	Standard deviation	Mean	Standard deviation	Mean	Standard deviation
London clearing banks	%	%	%	%	%	%
1975–77 [a]	50·04	0·91	83·71	0·96	43·83	1·94
1978–79 [b]	48·57	0·44	83·11	0·51	48·31	0·56
Scottish clearing banks						
1975–77 [a]	5·31	0·12	82·88	3·54	40·20	1·92
1978–79 [b]	5·20	0·07	79·16	1·08	43·62	1·18
Northern Ireland banks						
1975–77 [a]	1·90	0·35	97·64	0·23	50·47	2·35
1978 [c]	2·04	0·02	98·09	0·25	48·43	1·08
1979 [c]	1·67	0·05	98·32	0·15	39·04	3·10
Accepting houses						
1975–77 [a]	5·47	0·36	44·65	1·36	20·53	1·58
1978–79 [b]	5·67	0·26	45·78	1·61	22·49	1·07
Other British banks						
1975–77 [a]	19·49	1·57	47·07	3·45	18·11	1·42
1978–79 [b]	18·76	0·66	44·61	0·82	22·93	2·31
American banks						
1975–77 [a]	9·88	0·62	11·06	0·91	16·81	0·23
1978–79 [b]	10·53	0·52	13·09	0·68	16·45	1·19
Japanese banks						
1975–77 [a]	0·62	0·14	1·93	0·83	11·60	2·91
1978–79 [b]	0·65	0·09	2·15	0·14	12·15	1·58
Other overseas banks						
1975–77 [a]	6·02	0·54	11·02	0·66	22·97	0·72
1978–79 [b]	7·69	0·14	11·63	0·52	21·30	1·38
Consortium banks						
1975–77 [a]	1·04	0·11	7·71	1·53	16·19	3·36
1978–79 [b]	1·08	0·11	7·82	0·71	21·62	2·83

[a] Arithmetic means of monthly figures May 1975–December 1977 and standard deviations.

[b] Arithmetic means of monthly figures January 1978–October 1979 and standard deviations.

Sources of sterling deposits (as % of total sterling deposits)							
UK banking sector		Other UK		Overseas		Certificates of deposit	
Mean	Standard deviation	Mean	Standard deviation	Mean	Standard deviation	Mean	Standard deviation
%	%	%	%	%	%	%	%
3·81	0·85	88·06	1·60	4·68	0·38	3·45	0·75
6·40	0·65	83·78	0·84	5·44	0·36	4·39	0·70
1·88	0·65	92·34	1·26	1·82	0·23	3·98	1·15
3·45	0·82	89·83	1·11	2·09	0·06	4·62	1·24
18·67	3·69	55·62	2·77	25·72	1·16	0	–
26·40	1·46	49·31	1·42	24·29	0·52	0	–
34·88	4·53	57·87	2·61	7·24	2·87	0	–
21·72	1·78	65·93	1·86	6·82	0·55	5·53	1·59
24·60	2·85	64·97	3·69	6·74	1·44	3·62	0·61
39·46	2·11	39·61	2·29	10·61	0·55	9·84	2·84
42·01	2·22	39·77	0·81	11·37	0·37	6·85	1·68
38·40	3·16	30·99	1·59	8·44	1·40	22·17	2·42
40·07	3·60	32·73	2·00	8·35	1·40	18·85	2·86
65·94	5·66	26·76	4·11	6·47	1·85	0·87	0·66
65·43	2·09	25·19	1·58	8·38	1·52	1·25	0·73
33·34	2·06	31·52	1·42	24·65	1·49	10·50	1·06
41·03	2·33	27·15	2·00	22·81	2·49	8·90	1·21
49·39	4·12	26·55	3·50	12·55	2·53	11·63	3·45
57·80	3·14	19·31	2·81	16·77	2·55	6·13	1·55

[c] Arithmetic means of monthly figures January–December 1978 and January–October 1979 and standard deviations. Some accounting practices and arrangements were altered from January 1979.

Source: Calculated from statistics in *Bank of England Quarterly Bulletin*, March 1976, March 1977 and March 1978, tables 2/1–2/10; March, September and December 1979, tables 3/1–3/10.

proportion fell sharply in 1979 when the Irish Republic joined the European Monetary System. It is noteworthy that (apart from the change just indicated) the structure of deposits in the late 1970s was virtually the same as in the middle 1970s.

An important structural difference (not observable from statistics) between the clearing and Northern Ireland banks on the one hand and all remaining groups on the other is that the business of the former is predominantly 'retail' in character – each bank having a large number of deposits (and advances) on the books, most of which are small – whereas the latter are predominantly engaged in business of 'wholesale' nature – the units of deposits and loans being large but the numbers of accounts being small.[10] This structural difference explains some of the differences in methods and practices between the two categories of banks. In wholesale banking it is feasible to match liabilities and assets in terms of maturity, thus avoiding the necessity of holding low-yielding liquid assets on which retail banks must rely to maintain their ability to make payments to meet unexpected claims. But extensive matching is possible only if the banks can always obtain assets in a wide range of maturities to balance liabilities they have assumed, and also if they can always obtain deposits and other liabilities to finance the acquisition of attractive assets offered to them. Wholesale banks can achieve extensive matching only by large-scale operations in the interbank market – which explains the importance of interbank deposits for all 'secondary banks' – and in other parallel markets.

On the assets side, as in the case of deposits, sterling business is the preponderant business of London and Scottish clearing banks and of Northern Ireland banks and accounts for about half of the total business of accepting houses and other British banks; on the other hand, the assets of overseas and consortium banks are preponderantly foreign currency assets. This reflects, of course, the general practice of approximately matching liabilities by assets denominated in the same currency. Table 2 presents the structure of sterling assets in terms of average percentage ratios of the principal sterling assets to total sterling assets.

Several features of the asset structure deserve to be noted. In the first place, the average proportion of sterling assets held in the form of reserve assets (defined and described below, pp. 37–8) is similar for all groups of banks except consortium banks – this suggests that, in spite of great differences in the nature of their business, all banks attach roughly the same importance to holdings of very liquid assets which can be traded in the discount market. But, whereas London and Scottish clearing banks keep this ratio stable, other banks are prepared to allow significant fluctuations in it, both up and down.

All banks now operate in the interbank and CD markets and in other sterling parallel money markets. Assets arising out of these operations account for significant but not large, though somewhat variable, proportions of sterling assets of the London and Scottish clearing banks and for substantial proportions of non-clearing banks' sterling assets. The much greater use by non-clearing banks of the interbank, CD and other parallel markets as outlets for the employment of funds reflects, largely, their need to match wholesale assets and liabilities.

Advances to UK customers account for 45–50 per cent of total sterling assets of the clearing and Northern Ireland banks, and the proportions shown by American and Japanese banks are of a similar order. Accepting houses and consortium banks are at the other end of the scale, less than 30 per cent of their assets being advances to UK customers. Except in the case of Japanese banks, proportions vary very little.[11] Advances to overseas customers account for a significant proportion of sterling assets only in the case of London clearing banks; in all other cases the proportions are, somewhat surprisingly, small or very small.

British government stocks with more than one year to maturity seem to have little attractiveness for any of the groups of banks. In all cases they account for only small proportions of sterling assets, and these proportions are subject to significant variations. It appears probable that the banks hold short dated gilt-edged stocks as a secure source of reserve assets in the near future (when the passage of time brings them within one year of maturity) and longer dated gilt-edged securities as residual assets.

The structure of bank assets changed very little between the middle 1970s and the late 1970s. Differences in proportions shown in table 2 give a strong impression of reflecting adjustments to changes in conditions and circumstances rather than indicating structural changes.

Financial Markets in London

Efficient operation of a modern banking system requires the existence of

TABLE 2 *Structure of Sterling Assets of Banks in the UK*
(Principal sterling assets as % of total sterling assets) [a] [b]

	Total reserve assets		Loans to UK banking sector and holdings of CDs		Loans to local authorities, other market loans (incl. overseas) and holdings of non-reserve bills	
	Mean	Standard deviation	Mean	Standard deviation	Mean	Standard deviation
London clearing banks	%	%	%	%	%	%
1975–77 [c]	9·16	0·25	10·62	0·80	2·18	0·44
1978–79 [d]	8·92	0·31	10·38	1·65	1·84	0·62
Scottish clearing banks						
1975–77 [c]	8·45	0·25	10·14	1·74	2·20	0·41
1978–79 [d]	8·38	0·24	9·15	1·74	1·61	0·61
Northern Ireland banks						
1975–77 [c]	9·43	1·19	11·36	2·01	20·16	2·22
1978 [e]	9·29	0·17	9·92	0·75	19·76	0·82
1979 [e]	10·41	0·41	10·18	0·76	7·85	0·88
Accepting houses						
1975–77 [c]	8·32	1·20	27·11	2·42	17·79	1·61
1978–79 [d]	6·14	0·61	35·07	2·04	14·42	0·95
Other British banks						
1975–77 [c]	8·64	1·55	30·05	2·35	12·80	0·78
1978–79 [d]	6·18	0·58	34·38	2·66	10·77	0·97
American banks						
1975–77 [c]	9·10	0·66	29·56	2·38	9·63	1·13
1978–79 [d]	7·89	0·57	32·39	2·50	7·80	0·41
Japanese banks						
1975–77 [c]	9·34	1·37	16·25	4·27	4·76	1·05
1978–79 [d]	9·29	1·19	22·91	2·41	2·29	0·68
Other overseas banks						
1975–77 [c]	9·45	0·74	31·34	2·91	14·70	1·42
1978–79 [d]	8·10	0·97	35·45	1·67	13·17	1·39
Consortium banks						
1975–77 [c]	5·36	0·87	43·73	3·51	13·72	1·88
1978–79 [d]	4·44	0·34	42·09	5·47	13·88	1·81

Advances to UK customers		Advances to overseas customers		British government stocks with more than 1 year to maturity and undated	
Mean	Standard deviation	Mean	Standard deviation	Mean	Standard deviation
%	%	%	%	%	%
44·64	0·87	7·01	0·44	4·23	0·40
45·58	1·33	8·02	0·52	4·09	0·75
46·79	1·12	3·42	0·20	3·11	0·40
49·70	1·09	4·01	0·11	2·49	0·75
39·37	2·98	0·80	0·53	4·49	0·74
43·63	1·42	1·08	0·14	3·94	0·87
53·07	1·27	1·06	0·17	2·85	0·34
28·32	1·57	1·46	0·19	1·34	1·21
25·95	0·96	1·27	0·19	2·38	0·70
37·06	1·54	1·00	0·23	2·35	0·22
35·97	1·62	0·93	0·15	2·69	0·24
43·31	1·56	1·09	0·21	1·34	0·29
42·20	1·90	3·00	1·01	1·63	0·23
44·71	7·61	8·95	3·57	0·00	–
52·97	2·55	2·15	0·39	0·00	–
33·76	1·54	2·17	0·42	1·00	0·47
33·05	1·18	1·94	0·17	1·28	0·09
26·31	2·30	1·42	0·17	1·54	0·74
28·23	3·32	1·43	0·22	2·17	0·76

[a] 'Total sterling assets' include some miscellaneous assets in foreign currencies recorded together with miscellaneous sterling assets.

[b] Assets omitted from the table (notes and coin, special deposits, investments other than holdings of British Government stocks and miscellaneous assets) account for different proportions of total sterling assets of different groups of banks – higher for London and Scottish clearing banks than for other groups.

[c] Arithmetic means of monthly figures May 1975–Dec. 1977 and standard deviations.

[d] Arithmetic means of monthly figures Jan. 1978–Oct. 1979 and standard deviations.

[e] Arithmetic means of monthly figures Jan.–Dec. 1978 and Jan.–Oct. 1979 and standard deviations; presented separately because of changes in accounting arrangements from Jan. 1979.

Sources: Calculated from statistics in *Bank of England Quarterly Bulletin*, March 1976, March 1977 and March 1978, tables 2/2–2/10; March, September and December 1979, tables 3/2–3/10.

active and well organized financial markets. Until the second half of the 1950s there were in London only two financial markets directly relevant to operations of the banks: the long established discount market, and the gilt-edged market, a part of the Stock Exchange. Between that time and the end of the 1960s several new money markets came into being, grew rapidly and became a firmly established part of the financial environment. The principal new markets, now usually referred to as the parallel money markets, are:

the interbank market in sterling deposits
the market for temporary loans to (deposits with) UK local authorities
the market for finance house deposits
the secondary market for sterling certificates of deposit (CDs)
the Eurocurrency markets, among which the Eurodollar market is the largest and the most important
the secondary market for dollar certificates of deposit.

A detailed analysis of the organization, working and economic significance of the various financial markets is outside the scope of this work.[12] But a very brief indication of their main characteristics is necessary.

The traditional discount market consists of 11 discount houses, two discount brokers, and money trading departments of five banks. Although discount houses deal in several other assets, both sterling and foreign currency assets, the discount market is principally a market for bills – Treasury, local authority and other public sector bills and commercial bills – though short dated government securities (in respect of which discount houses perform a jobbing function) are also considered discount market assets.

Discount houses and other discount market institutions are dealers in bills and short bonds; that is to say, they buy bills and bonds from drawers and holders, hold them and sell them to willing buyers. The banks are the most important buyers of bills – London clearing banks do not themselves tender for Treasury bills and obtain all such bills from the discount market institutions, most of them from discount houses. All discount market institutions finance their asset holdings by borrowing funds, mainly from banks, at call and at short notice. Nearly all these loans are secured; i.e., bills and short bonds, and to a smaller extent other marketable assets owned by discount houses etc., are deposited with the lending banks.

Discount houses, but not other institutions, enjoy the unique privilege of access to the Bank of England in its capacity of lender of last resort. Thus, when the houses' asset-buying commitments and loan repayment obligations exceed the proceeds of sales of assets (including sales of bills to the special buyer who acts as agent of the Bank of England) and new market borrowing, they balance their books by obtaining last-resort loans from the Bank of England. The Bank never refuses to lend to discount houses but makes loans on terms of its own choosing, and these are normally penal in character. The most important asset-buying commitments arise as a result of the well established convention that discount houses as a group tender for the entire amount of Treasury bills offered at each Friday's tender. Because of this arrangement, discount houses often find themselves committed to buying a larger amount of bills than they can pay for out of funds obtainable from non-official sources. The Bank of England can assist them by instructing its agent to buy bills from discount houses or from the banks (which then lend to the houses) at ruling market rates, or it can force them to apply to the Bank's Discount Office for advances on which the Bank's minimum lending rate (a penal rate) is charged. Discount houses' loan repayment obligations are likely to arise – and to arise very suddenly, owing to the 'at call' nature of most of these loans – and at the same time new lending to the houses is likely to decrease, when private sector's payments to the government exceed the government's payments to the private sector: in such a case the banks lose cash (as their customers' cheques are presented by the Bank of England) and withdraw money from discount houses to restore their cash holdings. Again, the Bank of England can assist discount houses at market rates or force them to borrow from it on penal terms.

The Bank of England operates almost continuously in the discount market, buying Treasury bills and, sometimes, other bills or selling Treasury bills. The purpose of these operations is normally to prevent fluctuations in short-term interest rates which would result if imbalances in cash flows were not smoothed. By buying bills the Bank prevents increases in rates and by selling bills it counteracts downward adjustments in rates. But by limiting bill purchases, and therefore forcing discount houses to seek last resort loans, the Bank engineers a rise in the cost of marginal funds to discount houses and induces them to raise rates offered to other lenders and charged to customers wishing to sell assets to discount houses. To strengthen its hand in this respect the Bank always tries to make discount houses need official assistance. To this end it so determines the size of the Treasury bill issue in relation to other expected cash flows as to make discount houses commit themselves to buy more bills than they can pay for.

Between October 1972 and June 1978 the minimum lending rate (MLR) of the Bank of England was normally fixed every Friday according to the formula, MLR = average rate of discount on allotment of Treasury bills *plus* $\frac{1}{2}$ per cent, rounded to the nearest $\frac{1}{4}$ per cent above. The experiment of making MLR market-determined, i.e. making it follow market conditions as reflected by the avergae rate of discount at which Treasury bills were sold to tenderers, did not prove successful. Since June 1978 MLR, like the old Bank rate, is determined by the Court of Directors of the Bank of England, subject to approval by the Chancellor of the Exchequer, and is announced every Thursday. Thus, MLR now leads market rates instead of following them and, consequently, can be used as a policy instrument by the authorities.

The discount market occupies a very important place in the financial system for two reasons: (1) most discount market assets rank as reserve assets of banks and finance houses – thus, operations in the discount market affect the reserve position of the banks, and, consequently, their ability to make loans to customers; (2) it is through the discount market that the Bank of England supplies cash to the system, whether on its own initiative or in response to the system's action – these operations enable the Bank to influence interest rates. The position of the discount market is unique in both these respects.

The interbank market, the market in temporary loans to UK local authorities and that in finance house deposits have several important common features. All three are wholesale markets in clearing bank deposits; that is to say, lenders transfer to the borrowers sight claims on the clearing banks, and the units in which business is transacted are large.[13] Placements and borrowings are normally arranged by brokers, some of whom operate in all these markets and others of whom specialize. Brokers are in constant contact with potential lenders and borrowers and endeavour to match their requirements.[14] Loans in all three markets are unsecured and for this reason the name of the borrower is disclosed by the broker to the lender before the conclusion of the deal. This enables the lenders to set limits to their placements with particular borrowing institutions, depending on their size and standing.

In all three markets placements can be made for a wide range of maturities from overnight to 364 days, two years and five years in the local authority, finance house and interbank markets respectively. Loans (deposits) are made in these markets for specified periods or subject to notice and premature withdrawals are not normally allowed. Loans (deposits) are not negotiable. Interest rates ruling in these markets are determined by the interaction of demand and supply forces. Rates tend to be higher for longer maturities than for shorter ones,[15] and for a given maturity a little higher in the local authority than in the interbank market and a little higher still in the finance house market. Differences in interest rates on loans (deposits) of the same maturity are very fine because as assets these loans are very close substitutes for one another.

The Bank of England does not normally operate in parallel money markets but occasionally places funds in the interbank market and in the market for temporary loans to local authorities in order to prevent or relieve undue stringency and to influence interest rates in these markets. The Bank undertakes these operations on its own initiative; there is no formal lender of last resort to whom institutions operating in these markets could unquestionably turn when in difficulties. This does not unduly restrict the functioning of these markets because non-clearing banks and local authorities have stand-by credit arrangements with clearing banks.

The three markets take their names from the operators on the borrowing side, i.e., institutions taking deposits or soliciting loans. On this side the position is quite clear. It is less clear on the lending side. The banks are the preponderant lenders in the interbank market, but discount houses also place funds there and occasionally funds supplied from outside the banking sector are accepted on interbank terms. Banks are the principal lenders to local authorities and to finance houses, but discount houses, non-bank financial intermediaries and non-financial companies are also active suppliers of funds in these markets.

The secondary market in sterling certificates of deposit (CDs) is made by discount houses and by a few other dealers who buy these instruments from the issuing banks and from bank and non-bank holders, hold them and sell them to banks and other investors. It should be noted that the existence of a secondary market in CDs is the essential precondition of the banks' ability to issue them; it is the existence of the market in them that makes CDs easily negotiable in fact as well as in form, and it is easy negotiability that makes CDs more attractive than conventional deposits of the same maturity.

A certificate of deposit is a document certifying that a specified sum of money (minimum £50,000) has been deposited with the issuing bank for a definite period (three months to five years) at a stated rate of interest fixed for the whole period of currency of the certificate. The chief advantage of CDs as an asset lies in their negotiability: they can be sold at any time, but if not sold they yield interest to depositors at rates determined at the time of issue. Since prices in the secondary market depend on the current level of interest rates, pre-maturity sales of CDs may involve sellers in capital losses or yield capital gains to them.

Depositors appear to place considerable value on the advantage of negotiability: they are willing to supply funds to the banks by acquiring CDs for longer periods than they would be prepared to deposit funds in the ordinary way. Moreover, they are willing to buy CDs bearing a slightly lower rate of interest than they would demand on conventional time deposits of the same maturity. The ability to issue CDs has corresponding advantages to the banks: they obtain some funds for longer periods and some more cheaply than they could obtain by attracting conventional deposits. On the other hand holdings of CDs issued by other banks are remunerative and easily marketable assets, similar in character to holdings of bills and short bonds. Operations in CDs between banks and dealers and directly between banks have the same significance as interbank borrowing and lending, saleability of CDs constituting an additional advantage from the CDs buyers' point of view.

In normal times the operation of the CD market is simple. Discount houses and other dealers buy CDs from, and sell them to, holders and maintain the desired size and structure of their own portfolios by buying CDs from the issuing banks. They set their buying and selling prices to balance supply (including new issues) and demand. Problems are apt to arise if interest rates are expected to rise when the demand for CDs decreases and their supply to dealers increases. The resulting imbalance may put considerable strain on discount houses – their position as dealers in CDs requires them to but assets in the knowledge that if interest rates do rise these assets may well have to be carried at a loss. The banks have never committed themselves to support discount houses in such circumstances, but they provided support on several occasions by buying one another's CDs from discount houses to prevent undue growth of the houses' portfolios.

The Eurodollar market and other Eurocurrency markets[16] are wholesale, interbank markets in deposits with banks in the countries in whose currencies these deposits are denominated. These markets are international in nature and in physical location; i.e., Eurocurrency markets in London are sections of these international markets.[17]

Eurocurrency markets provide to UK banks facilities for placing and taking (borrowing) foreign currency balances for a wide range of maturities – overnight to five years. Thus, they resemble in character and significance the interbank market in sterling deposits. Their existence greatly facilitates matching foreign currency assets and liabilities in an economic manner and therefore encourages the banks to develop foreign currency business to the advantage of their customers, with beneficial effects on the UK balance of payments and at a profit to themselves.

The secondary market in dollar certificates of deposit is made by the discount houses together with London offices of a few American security dealers. This market operates in the same manner as that in sterling CDs. American banks in London normally stand ready to provide support to discount houses if the latter experience difficulties as a result of operations in dollar CDs.

Bank Operations in Financial Markets

Traditionally, the functions of the discount houses have long been to supply income-earning but highly liquid assets to the banks and to provide the banks with facilities for carrying out, on demand, adjustments in the volume and structure of bank liquidity. These traditional functions are now largely performed by the parallel sterling markets, particularly the interbank sterling market.* But the discount market retains a very special position: apart from the authorities, it is the principal supplier of eligible reserve assets to the banks. Thus, although some transactions between banks and discount houses are in

* Unless a bank has a surplus of reserves it cannot use money at call with the discount houses for general adjustments in liquidity. If money at call withdrawn from the market is used to buy other reserve assets the overall reserve position is unchanged; if it is used for other purposes the reserve position worsens.

assets that do not rank as reserve assets (e.g., loans at short notice, non-eligible bills, CDs and government securities with more than a year to maturity), in a large majority of cases bank operations in the discount market are operations in reserve assets, i.e., operations that affect the size and composition of bank reserves.

The banks acquire reserve assets by placing money at call with the discount houses and other listed discount market institutions and by buying from them eligible bills and government securities with less than one year to final maturity. They can reduce their holdings of reserve assets by withdrawing call money from the market and by reducing purchases of bills and very short government bonds below the level of current maturities of these assets.

The fact that assets generated in bank operations in the discount market are reserve assets gives rise to the possibility that the banking sector might be able to use these operations to create additional reserves for itself. This problem will be examined in depth in chapter 3.

London clearing banks lend to discount houses and pay them for bills, etc., by placing claims upon themselves (sight deposits) at the disposal of the discount houses. The houses draw on these clearing bank deposits to make their own payments. It follows, of course, that an individual clearing bank can place additional funds in the discount market only if it can meet the resulting claims on it as they are presented at the clearing. Non-clearing banks lend to discount houses by transferring to them balances (deposits) that they hold with London clearing banks. As a result of such transfers non-clearing banks substitute money at call (a reserve asset) for balances with clearing banks (which do not rank as reserve assets); London clearing banks must meet claims on them* at the clearing while reducing their deposit liabilities by the same amounts.[18]

Banks operate in the discount market in order to adjust their holdings of reserve assets as necessary or desirable in view of changes in their balance sheet positions brought about by the transaction of normal business and of other relevant changes in the monetrary and financial situation. In the normal course of day-to-day business some banks experience an inflow of funds (balanced, of course, by an increase in deposits or other liabilities), whereas other banks suffer an outflow of funds and a fall in deposits. Both groups must make appropriate

* Claims resulting from the use by discount houses of funds lent them by non-clearing banks.

adjustments in the volume and composition of holdings of reserve assets,[19] which they normally accomplish by operations in the discount market. Discount houses act as intermediaries, in this case repaying money at call to some banks and increasing their borrowing from others, without experiencing any particular strain. But if, as a result of official policy measures or of external influences, the banking system as a whole either finds it necessary to withdraw money at call from the market or to increase placements in the market, discount houses find themselves under strain, and the nature of the strain and the houses' reactions to it have important effects on interest rates, on the availability of funds, on investors' expectations, etc.

All UK banks operate extensively in parallel sterling money markets, supplying funds to other participants and drawing funds from them by borrowing or by requiring repayment of outstanding market loans falling due. For an individual bank the general object of operations in parallel markets (on both sides) is to adjust the size and structure of its balance sheet so as to establish and maintain the most favourable position.

The principal parallel markets supply assets of very high quality and offer them for a wide and very finely graded range of maturities. Thus, the banks can place funds in these markets for several different purposes: to employ temporarily surplus funds; to ensure the availability of funds in the future when they are expected to be needed (in most cases the purpose of these operations is to match deposits or other liabilities which, in view of their maturities or for other reasons, cannot be matched by loans to customers, but they may also represent the use of funds deliberately acquired in excess of current requirements when interest rates are low but are expected to rise); to acquire assets whose yield and other characteristics make them attractive in themselves, given the banks' desired structure of assets. In so far as placements for very short periods are concerned, parallel markets provide the same facilities as the discount market but offer them, usually, on more attractive terms. On the other hand, assets generated in parallel markets, unlike most discount market assets, do not rank as reserve assets; nor can they be shifted on to the Bank of England as lender of last resort. By providing facilities for longer-term investment of funds parallel markets increase the diversification of first-class assets and thus facilitate the maintenance of the most appropriate asset structure by banks and other suppliers of funds.

Parallel markets provide individual banks with facilities to raise funds. By borrowing in the interbank market, by issuing new CDs or selling other banks' CDs to dealers, and by requiring repayment of funds previously lent in the interbank market or in other parallel markets, a bank can at any time obtain funds independently of, and in addition to, the current flow of deposits. Consequently, disbursements – loans to customers, repayment of deposits or discharge of other liabilities – need not be directly related to, or constrained by, the current inflow of funds or undesired sales of other assets. The existence of parallel markets enables individual banks to pursue freer and more flexible lending and investment policies.

Transactions in parallel markets take the form of transfers of sight deposits with London clearing banks from the suppliers of funds to the recipients.* Deposits with London clearing banks are not, of course, eligible reserve assets of the banks holding them. But they can be turned into reserve assets by using them, for example, to make call loans to discount houses or to buy Treasury bills from the houses. It is extremely important to note that, by borrowing in the interbank market, banks put themselves in a position of being able to increase their holdings of reserve assets much more than they need to increase them to support the rise in eligible liabilities resulting directly from interbank borrowing. Thus, they can increase lending because they have means to meet claims to which new lending gives rise, whatever form these claims may take.

Lending (placing) funds in parallel markets causes an outflow of reserves from the funds-supplying banks. It has already been said that a clearing bank lends by putting a deposit at the disposal of the borrower. The latter's disbursements (use of the loan) generate claims on the lending clearing bank; these claims are presented by other clearing banks and are settled by transfers of balances with the Bank of England. Lending in parallel markets, just like other lending, causes an outflow of reserves from the lending banks. Lending in parallel markets is a deliberate action of the lending bank taken to employ funds that have flowed in normally in the form of balances with the Bank of England. In

* If a London clearing bank lends to another bank it creates a sight deposit with itself in favour of the recipient. If a London clearing bank borrows from another bank or withdraws funds from parallel markets it acquires either claims on other clearing banks, which when cleared increase its balance with the Bank of England, or claims upon itself, which are thereby automatically redeemed.

such a case the fact that lending causes an outflow of reserves is not a problem. But demands for repayment of funds borrowed in the interbank market cause an outflow of reserves that may be uncompensated by a simultaneous inflow. In such a case the reserve-losing bank must sell non-reserve assets,[20] obtaining in exchange either balances with the Bank of England (from other clearing banks) or claims on other clearing banks (from non-clearing banks) which the latter settle by surrendering balances with the Bank of England.

Parallel market lending by a non-clearing bank takes the form of a transfer of deposit from the lending bank's account with one clearing bank to the borrower's account with another clearing bank. The lending non-clearing bank reduces its deposit with its clearing bank and increases its other parallel market assets; its own reserves are unaffected at this stage but its clearing bank experiences an outflow of reserves. It appears that operations of non-clearing banks impose pressure on the reserves of 'their' clearing banks. But this 'pressure' is of the same nature as the effects of payments made by a clearing bank's ordinary customers to customers of other clearing banks. As in the case of a clearing bank, it can be presumed that placements in parallel markets are made when resources are available, i.e. when the non-clearing bank's balance with its clearing bank has risen – the counterpart of the rise in that clearing bank's deposits being an inflow of reserve assets (balances with the Bank of England).

If a non-clearing bank is required to repay an interbank loan the effect is to reduce its working balance with the clearing bank below the level that it is necessary to maintain. The working balance must therefore be rebuilt and this can be achieved in several ways. The non-clearing bank may withdraw money at call from the discount houses and use the proceeds (discount houses' cheques on clearing banks or on the Bank of England) to increase the deposit with its clearing bank – in this case the repayment of an interbank loan reduces reserves of the non-clearing bank but the reserve position of the clearing bank concerned is unaffected. The non-clearing bank pressed for repayment of an interbank loan may itself withdraw funds from parallel markets, thus obtaining claims on clearing banks from its debtors – in this case the non-clearing bank reduces its non-reserve assets to balance a fall in its liabilities, the reserve position of its clearing bank is again unaffected, and the reserve problem is shifted on to other banks in the system. Finally, the non-clearing bank in question may use stand-by credit facilities normally provided by its clearing bank – in this case it rearranges its liabilities, its reserves are unchanged, and the clearing bank concerned accepts the reserve problem as a counterpart of an increase in its (presumably profitable) interbank lending.[21]

Operations in the CD market (but not issues of CDs to holders outside the banking sector) have the same effects on the reserves of the banks involved as corresponding transactions in the interbank market. (Sales of CDs to other banks are equivalent to interbank borrowing; purchases of CDs are equivalent to interbank lending.)

Fund-raising operations in the local authority and finance house markets take the form of obtaining repayment of funds previously placed there. The proceeds accrue to the funds-withdrawing banks in a form (clearing bank deposits) that makes possible immediate acquisition of reserve assets if the banks in question need to strengthen their reserves, or of non-reserve assets more attractive than parallel market placements, e.g. loans to customers, or an immediate discharge of liabilities of all kinds.[22]

Operations in the interbank market enable banks to redistribute loanable resources from those whose resources exceed lending opportunities to those whose lending opportunities are greater than their own resources. A similar redistribution occurs as a result of operations in CDs to the extent that some banks' purchases of CDs are matched by other banks' sales; it also occurs in so far as new placements of bank funds in the local authority and finance house markets match other banks' withdrawals of funds from these markets.

Redistribution of loanable resources makes it possible for the banking system as a whole to increase the total volume of lending. This, however, increases the total volume of deposits and therefore of eligible liabilities. It follows that the scope of effective redistribution of resources is limited by the availability of reserve assets either from excess holdings of these assets within the system or from outside. Likewise, the ability of the banks to avoid reducing their lending or to limit such reduction depends on the availability of reserve assets from within the system or from outside. These important problems will be discussed in later chapters.

CHAPTER TWO

Competition for Deposits

The essence of banking, and, indeed, of many other types of financial intermediation, is the acceptance of deposits from one group of customers and the lending of funds so obtained to another group of customers. Moreover, until fairly recently it was true to say that, apart from special cases, deposits had to be obtained before loans could be made; in other words, a bank was visualized as passively taking deposits when they were offered by customers and then seeking appropriate outlets for the employment of resources deposited with it.

Until the early 1960s the view of banking summarized above constituted a fair representation of the practice of most banks in Britain. In the 1960s, however, important changes and innovations were introduced and spread widely and quickly. The most important structural changes were the rapid growth of secondary, wholesale banks, both British and foreign, and the development of the interbank market in sterling funds and of other parallel money markets. Among the many important innovations, one with very far-reaching consequences was the acceptance of direct interbank borrowing/lending as a normal feature of banking business. The need for transactions of this type arose because of the wholesale nature of the business of secondary banks and the consequent difficulties that individual banks experienced in matching the inflow of deposits to them with their lending opportunities. The interbank market developed because it provided facilities for solving these difficulties in a way attractive to all concerned: banks with surpluses of resources became able to employ them safely and remuneratively, whereas banks short of resources could avoid being forced to lose profitable lending opportunities because of temporary lack of funds.

Until 1971 the clearing banks did not participate in the interbank market and did not operate in other parallel markets. After 1971, however, they became active and, because of their size, very important operators in all parallel markets.

Liability Management

The development of parallel money markets, in particular of the interbank market and of the market in sterling certificates of deposit, made it possible for all banks to adopt, or at least occasionally to resort to, the technique that has become known as 'liability management'. The essence of this technique is that, instead of treating the existing volume of deposits and other liabilities as determining the volume of assets that it can hold, a bank attempts to adjust the volume of liabilities to the desired total of assets or to the desired expansion in the volume of assets. In other words, liability management reverses the traditional banking sequence: instead of first obtaining deposits and *then* making loans, the banks make loans as opportunities occur and then seek resources for them.

It goes without saying that the technique of liability management is possible only if large funds can be raised without delay. Thus, it clearly could not be applied before the 1960s, when there was really only one source of bank deposits: individual economic units – households and firms. The banks were not entirely passive with respect to deposits in those days. Advertising, expansion of branch network, special facilities for students, etc., aimed, at least partly, at attracting deposits. These methods, however, could only produce effects in the long run. Similarly, the manipulation of the rate of interest paid on deposits (a method that was not used by the clearing banks in the 1950s and 1960s) could not be expected to induce quick response from bank customers other than financial institutions. Thus, it was only when active parallel money markets developed and became firmly established that liability management became a feasible banking technique. Secondary banks applied it in the 1960s, but its use did not spread to the clearing banks until after the introduction of competition and credit control.

There are several types of operations that the banks can use to increase their liabilities, at the same time obtaining command of loanable resources. In the first place, banks seeking funds can borrow them in the interbank market, i.e. from other banks, those which, for reasons of their own, wish to employ some of their resources in interbank loans. Second, banks short of funds can obtain them by issuing certificates of deposit. To the extent that CDs are sold to dealers (discount houses) who finance their purchases out of funds borrowed from banks, or if they are sold directly to other banks, the issue of CDs is a substitute for interbank borrowing – issuers of CDs obtain funds from other banks. CDs issued to non-bank holders are paid for by surrendering the buyers' deposits with their own banks to the issuers, so that in fact the latter obtain resources from other banks. But in so far as the buyers of CDs would otherwise have bought securities from the authorities, the increase in liabilities of the banks that expanded their issues of CDs represents retention of resources within the banking system which would have left it if new CDs had not been issued. Third, large (over £50,000) deposits for fixed periods are placed on terms negotiated individually between the banks and the depositors. The depositors are mainly financial institutions and large non-financial companies with extensive banking and market contacts. A bank seeking funds can attract deposits of this type by offering better terms than those offered by other banks. As in the case of CDs issued to non-bank holders, banks that succeed in attracting wholesale deposits obtain resources mostly from other banks but may cause retention in the banking system of some funds that would otherwise have left it. Fourth, banks may obtain funds from other banks by requiring repayment of interbank loans or by selling other banks' CDs from holdings. In the ordinary sense of the term the liabilities of the banks undertaking these operations are not affected, but the fact that their eligible liabilities increase[1] provides a justification for treating these operations as pertaining to liability management.[2]

With the exception of demanding repayment of maturing interbank loans, operations described above can be successfully carried out only if agreement is reached with the other parties concerned. It is necessary to offer appropriate inducements to those other parties, and these take the form of interest rate offers attractive in relation to yields obtainable on other uses of funds.

The attractiveness of liability management to a bank with opportunities to expand loans or to a bank faced with withdrawal of deposits or other resources is obvious.

In the former case, if and as long as the cost of raising additional resources (liabilities) – principally the rate of interest that must be paid to obtain them – is lower than the weighted average rate of interest on reserve and non-reserve assets that the bank desires to acquire, liability management operations can be confidently expected to increase the bank's profits. Furthermore, if it is assumed (not unreasonably) that the cost of raising additional resources tends to rise as their amount increases and that the yield of assets, allowing for risks, etc., decreases or remains unchanged, the problem is essentially that of marginal cost/marginal revenue relationship. Thus, the technique of liability management enables the banks to approach their optimum size much more closely than they can do if they adopt a passive attitude to liabilities.

In the case of withdrawal of deposits, the problem is that of comparing the cost of raising additional resources in order to maintain unchanged the existing asset holdings and the loss of revenue that must follow the reduction in asset holdings in line with the fall in deposits; as long as the former is lower than the latter, liability management is profitable.

An individual bank can successfully use the technique of liability management so long as the margin between lending rates and interest rates that must be paid to attract additional deposits is wide enough to cover other costs involved and provide adequate compensation for extra risks. If, however, liability management is in general use in the banking system the success of one bank in attracting deposits necessarily involves deposit losses for other banks. These banks react by intensifying their efforts to attract deposits with the result that strong interbank competition for deposits develops. This competition for deposits has very important effects on the monetary situation and on the implementation of monetary policy. These effects are examined in the next section.

Competition for Deposits and the Reserve Position of the Banks

When a bank succeeds in attracting a deposit the counterpart of the increase in liabilities is an accrual of assets. If the bank concerned is a clearing bank the accrual of assets takes the form of a rise in that bank's balance with the Bank of England (a reserve asset which bears no interest but which can be immediately turned into interest-bearing reserve assets, e.g. money at call); if it is a non-clearing bank it normally acquires a clearing bank deposit, not itself a reserve asset but one that can be turned into reserve assets by using it to place money at call with discount houses or by buying Treasury bills, etc. Thus, generally, a bank that succeeds in attracting a deposit experiences at the same time an increase in the holdings of reserve assets. It follows therefore that interbank competition for deposits is also competition among banks for reserve assets. The importance of this aspect of the problem is very far-reaching. Because of it the technique of liability management may be used – and, under certain conditions, successfully used – by the banks to strengthen their reserve position and thus to make possible an increase in the rate of expansion of their business, or to reduce the weakening of their reserve position caused by official action, thus lessening the magnitude of the consequential contractionary adjustment of their deposits and assets.

Individual banks can attract deposits and reserve assets easily by drawing them from one another. To the extent that this occurs deposits and reserves are redistributed within the banking system, but their aggregate amounts in the system remain unchanged. However, simultaneous bidding for deposits by all banks can bring about increases in these aggregates if it affects transactions involving the government or the overseas sector – in the latter case, usually involving the government indirectly. More specifically, interbank competition for deposits can give rise to increases in aggregate bank deposits and in aggregate reserves of the banking system if it diverts private sector funds from the government to the banks or if it attracts foreign funds to the banks, causing a fall in government borrowing from the overseas sector. These changes in the flow of funds cause aggregate bank deposits to rise; the increase in government borrowing from the banking sector (needed to balance decreases in the borrowing from the private and overseas sectors) increases the supply of reserve assets to the banks.

Interbank competition for deposits causes the relevant interest rates to rise; CD rates, rates on wholesale term deposits with banks, and rates ruling in the interbank market all tend to be strongly and immediately affected. Increases in these rates are very likely to alter rate relativities; in particular, they are likely to change the relationships between CD rates and rates on wholesale bank deposits on the one hand and the Treasury bill rate and gilt-edged rates at the short end of the spectrum on the other. Thus, investment in assets supplied by the banks becomes more attractive relatively to investment in short-term instruments of public sector debt. This changes the structure of the supply of funds – instead of flowing to the government, they flow to the banks. And the government must increase its borrowing from the banks to balance the decrease in its borrowing from non-bank economic units in the private sector.

In terms of the banks' balance sheets the diversion of funds from the government to the banking system takes the form of retention by the banks of private sector deposits which the depositors would otherwise transfer to the government in exchange for interest bearing public sector debt. The banks retain these deposits (which, originally, are likely to be in the form of current accounts or seven-day deposits) by inducing depositors to exchange them for high yielding term deposits and CDs. At the same time the fall in private sector lending to the government causes government payments to the private sector to exceed receipts from the private sector (or increases the size of the excess of government payments over receipts); the excess of government payments to the private sector generates an equal amount of new bank deposits, and the rise in deposits is balanced by the acquisition by the banking sector of public sector debt, partly in the form of eligible reserve assets. When the banks' reserve position is tight a substantial proportion of any increase in government borrowing from the banking sector is likely to take the form of issues of reserve assets to the banks – the government can always borrow from the banking sector but it cannot choose the classes of assets it issues to the banks: it must supply assets that the banks desire to buy.

There are indications that changes and adjustments outlined above actually took place in 1972 and 1973. The banks competed very keenly for deposits, and as a result of this competition interest rates on certificates of deposit and on fixed-term conventional deposits with banks followed a very pronounced upward trend throughout these two years. Moreover, the CD rate tended to rise sharply in relation to the Treasury bill rate and to (redemption) yields on short dated gilt-edged stocks. For most of 1973 the rate of interest on three-month CDs was higher than

FIGURE 1

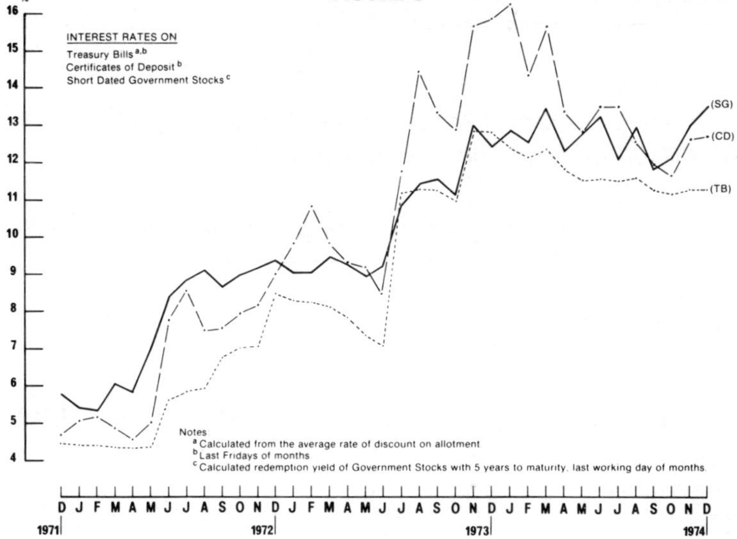

FIGURE 2

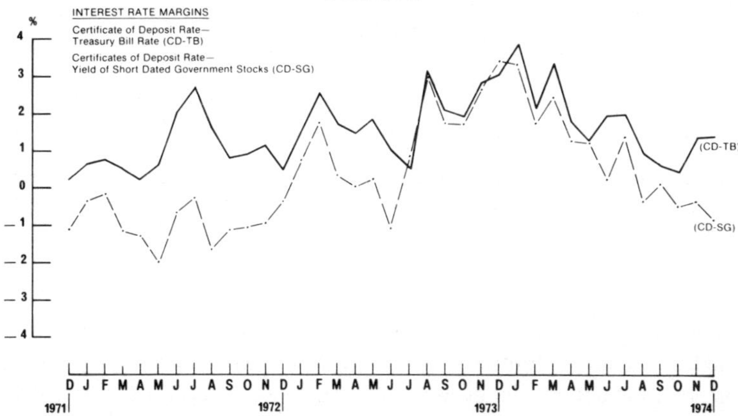

the yield on gilt-edged stocks with the maturity of five years (figures 1 and 2).[3]

A group of economic units very likely to adjust the pattern of their demand for assets in response to changes in relative yields are financial institutions other than banks. In the context of the present discussion it is particularly interesting to observe portfolio behaviour of these institutions in respect of holdings of bank deposits (including CDs) and holdings of government stocks.[4]

TABLE 3 *Increases in Holdings of Bank Deposits and of Government Stocks by Financial Institutions other than Banks*

	1970	1971	1972	1973	1974	1975
£ million						
Additions to bank deposits	278	182	918	1,016	871	−629
Acquisitions of government stocks	320	1,432	418	694	293	3,309
Total identified acquisitions of financial assets	3,203	4,641	6,346	5,556	4,509	8,375
As % of total identified acquisition of assets						
Additions to bank deposits	8·7	3·9	14.5	18·3	19·3	−7·5
Acquisitions of government stocks	10·0	30·7	6·6	12·5	6·5	39·5

Source: Flow of Funds and Sector Financing tables, *Bank of England Quarterly Bulletin*, June 1974, June 1975, June 1978 and subsequently revised figures communicated by the Bank of England to the author (reproduced with the Bank's permission).

Table 3 shows clearly that, in both 1972 and 1973, when CD rates were rising relatively to yields on short-dated government stocks, non-bank financial institutions made large additions to their deposits with banks using substantial proportions of new resources for this purpose. On the other hand, their appetite for government stocks was weaker than previously. These figures are fully consistent with the proposition that changes in the structure of interest rates that occurred in 1972 and 1973 induced an adjustment in non-bank financial institutions' demand for assets, strengthening their desire to hold bank deposits and weakening their wish to hold government stocks. Quarterly figures for 1972 and 1973, although less clear-cut, suggest the same conclusion. On the other hand, while the figures for 1974 as a whole appear to tell the same story, quarterly data present a more complex picture. Disregarding the first quarter of 1974 because of the severe distortions caused by the three-day week, etc., it can be observed that in the second quarter non-bank financial institutions ran down bank deposits and made substantial acquisition of government stocks although interest rate comparisons still favoured CDs. It is possible that the fact that interest rates have been falling since the beginning of the year, combined with the approach of the date at which supplementary special deposits scheme would become operative, created expectations of further and sharper falls in rates, thus increasing the relative attractiveness of gilt-edged stocks. In the last two quarters of 1974, when the yields of short-dated stocks exceeded the CD rate, non-bank financial institutions added substantially to their bank deposits and, in the last quarter, disposed of gilt-edged stocks. A possible explanation may be that gilt-edged and other rates were expected to rise – in fact, short gilt-edged rates rose steadily from September, and CD rates from October, until the end of the year.

Sharp increases in interest rates offered by the banks on CDs and wholesale term deposits often tend to attract foreign funds.[5] In the first instance these funds flow into the UK in the form of claims on foreign banks denominated in foreign currencies and must be converted into sterling either in the foreign exchange market or by selling them directly to the Exchange Equalization Account (EEA). In the former case, sterling deposits of UK banks' non-resident customers increase but deposits of home customers decrease (having been used to buy foreign currencies from non-residents); bank reserves are unaffected. But UK residents' current demand for foreign currencies is independent of the inflow of foreign funds; it follows that in the absence of that inflow deposits of domestic customers would have decreased (because they would have been transferred to the EEA in payment for foreign currencies) and the banks would have lost a corresponding amount of reserves. If foreign currencies are sold directly to the EEA, non-resident deposits with UK banks rise and the banks acquire sterling cash supplied by the EEA. In both cases bank deposits (sterling) and assets are greater than they would have been if foreign funds had not been attracted. Non-resident sterling deposits are not included in the UK stock of money, and so an increase in them does not affect the rate of monetary growth. But to the extent that the rise in these deposits (at least partly balanced by a rise in reserves) is used by the banks to increase lending to UK residents, new resident deposits are generated and these deposits constitute an addition to the stock of money (sterling M3).

The inflow of foreign funds either reduces sterling receipts of the EEA[6] or increases its sterling payments. In both cases the ability of the EEA to provide finance to the Exchequer decreases; indeed, in the latter case the Exchequer may have to provide sterling finance to the EEA. In other words, if the banking sector attracts foreign funds the contribution made by the overseas sector to the financing of the public sector borrowing requirement decreases and (given public sector borrowing from the private sector) the government must increase the borrowing from the banks. And this results in an increase in bank deposits balanced by increases in the banks' holdings of reserve (and other) assets; i.e., it results in a rise in the stock of money and in the creation of a base for further monetary expansion.

The banks' purpose in striving to attract deposits is to maintain the rate of expansion of lending or to reduce it less than would be necessary if they responded to reserve pressure in what before 1971 was considered to be the 'normal' manner. As a result of such action eligible liabilities of the banking system grow, and unless additional reserve assets flow into the banking system, e.g. because of changes in the structure of government borrowing already described, the reserve position of the banking system as a whole must become progressively tighter. Banks that find themselves with inadequate reserves then claim repayment of interbank loans, offer other banks' CDs for sale and present maturing CDs to issuing banks for encashment; at the same time, banks on which these claims are made try to borrow in the interbank market and to sell CDs so as to meet their obligation without themselves suffering major outflows of reserves. A severely stringent situation, possibly bordering on the chaotic, may develop in financial markets greatly impeding the working of the financial mechanism with widespread and damaging economic consequences. The authorities have then little choice but to assist the system by an injection of reserve assets, although such assistance necessarily weakens the effects of the policy of monetary restraint which in the authorities' view remains necessary. This is what occurred between January and March 1973, when the Bank of England found it necessary to buy over £200 million commercial bills from discount houses to relieve reserve stringency which developed as the banks attempted to avoid contractionary adjustment following calls for special deposits in December 1972 and January 1973. Again, in August 1973 the Bank had to supply £100 million of reserves to the system.[7]

It follows from the foregoing that if the practice of liability management leads to keen interbank competition for deposits its effects may cause an increase in the supply of reserve assets to the banking system through one or more of the channels described above. In other words, the practice of liability management tends to weaken the ability of the authorities to control the reserve base of the banking system and, therefore, their control over monetary aggregates quantitatively related to the reserve base of the banks. The possibility of an adverse impact of liability management on the efficacy of monetary control was recognized by the authorities in 1973: the supplementary special deposits scheme was devised to damp down interbank competition for resources[8] and thus to limit its adverse effects.

One other effect of keen interbank competition for deposits (and other resources) must be noted. Competitive bidding for resources is immediately reflected in increases in interest rates on CDs and on fixed-term conventional deposits and in interbank market rates. But the banks' lending rates, being tied to base rates that are governed by general market conditions, often tend to lag behind. Severe distortions to the pattern of rates may then arise, CD and other money market rates being higher than lending rates applicable to first-class borrowers. It then becomes possible for bank customers who have or can obtain overdraft facilities or short-term advances to arbitrage between bank loans and certificates of deposit – using the proceeds of the former to acquire the latter.

From the point of view of the bank issuing CDs it does not matter that the buyer of CDs finances his purchase by borrowing from another bank. The issuer of CDs obtains claims on another bank which it can immediately turn into eligible reserve assets; its reserve position improves, and it can acquire (or need not dispose of) high yielding non-reserve assets.[9]

From the point of view of the banking system as a whole, arbitrage transactions are inferior to direct interbank borrowing as a method of increasing the utilization of resources of the banking system. An interbank loan increases eligible liabilities of the borrowing bank but reduces by the same amount those of the lending bank[10] – eligible liabilities of the banking system are unchanged. Reserves are transferred from the lending bank to the borrowing bank but the total reserve base of the system remains the same. In the case of arbitrage, eligible liabilities of the banks issuing CDs increase but eligible liabilities of the banks that lend to finance the purchase of CDs do not decrease. Thus, there is a net increase in the eligible liabilities of the system but its reserve base is unchanged. Consequently, the reserve position of the banking system worsens. At the end of 1973 the banks took action to stop arbitrage operations by their customers: they agreed to charge money market rates on overdrafts by customers able to lend in the money market – other banks, finance houses, local authorities and some other customers.

Arbitrage operations cause an increase in non-bank holdings of certificates that are a component of the stock of money (M3). The increase in the stock of money so generated is, however, merely a statistical phenomenon. It does not indicate an increase in the availability of money for spending.[11] Arbitrage operations cause a spurious element to enter into the stock of money statistics: when these operations occur the recorded rate of growth of the stock of money (M3) is distorted upwards, and when unwinding of arbitrage positions takes place statistics understate the true rate of monetary growth. These distortions reduce the value of M3 statistics as an indicator of the monetary situation and of monetary trends.

CHAPTER THREE

The Competition and Credit Control System

Introduction

The competition and credit control system was introduced in September 1971 following a thorough review and reappraisal of the objects and techniques of monetary policy by the Treasury and the Bank of England and after consultations with the banks.

The system has two broad aims: (1) to ensure that the available supply of financial resources is allocated to various uses by the free operation of the price mechanism; (2) to ensure that the authorities can – by appropriately influencing market conditions and thus inducing changes in market behaviour in response to the alterations in market conditions – exercise firm control over the size or the rate of growth of the stock of money and over other monetary aggregates.

The price mechanism can operate efficiently only in a genuinely competitive environment. To establish such an environment the introduction of the competition and credit control system was accompanied by important changes in operational practices of the banks and in methods of implementation of monetary measures by the authorities. All conventional links between interest rates and all cartel arrangements on interest rates were abolished, and official quantitative restrictions on bank and finance house lending (which constituted the principal instrument of monetary control in the 1950s and 1960s) were discontinued. Moreover, the policy of supporting the gilt-edged market by buying securities in response to requests by sellers had already been abandoned since May 1971 with the effect of making gilt-edged interest rates market-determined and relieving the authorities of the need to supply cash to the system whenever gilt-edged prices tended to fall. The authorities continued to stand ready to buy, at the request of sellers, gilt-edged stock with not more than one year to final maturity. Needless to say, the new dispensation in no way affected the right of the authorities to buy long-term stock, to sell it and to facilitate exchanges of stock on their own initiative and at prices of their own choosing.

On the operational level the keynotes of the competition and credit control scheme are generality and uniformity of treatment. All banks, clearing and non-clearing alike and including foreign banks operating in the United Kingdom, are subject to the same reserve ratio requirements, and similarly the obligation to place special deposits at a common rate or rates applies to all of them.[1] Very similar requirements and obligations apply to finance houses,[2] and eventually Trustee Savings Banks and the National Giro will be brought into the system.

The generality and uniformity of the arrangements have made it possible for the clearing banks to undertake many activities from which they previously refrained because they were subject to requirements and control that did not apply to other banks. Thus, under the competition and credit control system all banks and finance houses can compete freely with one another and with other financial institutions both in borrowing and in lending.

The competition and credit control scheme was established by agreement between the authorities (the Treasury and the Bank of England) and the banks, discount houses and finance houses. Thus, strictly speaking, the compliance of the banks, etc., with the rules of the scheme is voluntary. This, of course, is the continuation of the British banking tradition. But it must be borne in mind that the Bank of England has sufficient financial powers and, in the last resort, legal powers under section 4 of the Bank of England Act, 1946, to ensure that the rules and obligations are universally regarded as binding.

The Formal Structure of the Competition and Credit Control System

The formal structure of the system is very simple and can be described under three headings: (1) reserve requirements, (2) special deposits, and (3) supplementary special deposits.

Reserve Requirements

All banks in the United Kingdom have agreed to maintain, day by day, reserve ratios, i.e. ratios between eligible reserve assets and eligible liabilities, of not less than $12\frac{1}{2}$ per cent, and finance houses (except those with eligible liabilities not exceeding £5 million) have similarly agreed to maintain reserve ratios of not less than 10 per cent.

The following categories of liabilities have been designated as 'eligible liabilities' (cf. *Bank of England Quarterly Bulletin*, December 1971, pp. 482–4).

(1) Sterling deposits of an original maturity of two years and under from UK non-bank customers and from overseas customers (except the reporting banks' overseas offices), and funds due to customers or third parties temporarily held in suspense accounts (except credits in the course of transmission). Deposits placed for more than two years without provision for pre-maturity withdrawal are considered to have the character of loan capital rather than deposit liabilities and for this reason are excluded. The period of two years is of necessity somewhat arbitrary. The funds temporarily in suspense accounts are included because they are expected to be credited to deposits within a short period of time.
(2) All sterling deposits (irrespective of term) from banks in the UK *less* sterling claims on (mostly deposits with) other UK banks.*
(3) All sterling certificates of deposit issued (irrespective of term) *less* holdings of other banks' CDs.

Categories (2) and (3) of eligible liabilities concern, of course, interbank claims and counterclaims. Only net liabilities on interbank deposits and net CD liabilities count as eligible liabilities because a bank that places deposits with other banks or buys other banks' CDs passes to those other banks resources it had obtained. By doing so it enables the recipients of funds to use them for lending outside the banking system. It is no more than fair that the obligation to count funds as eligible liabilities and therefore to hold reserves in respect of these funds is imposed on the ultimate user banks and not on those that act as in-

* In the case of finance houses amounts borrowed from banks are excluded from eligible liabilities.

termediaries within the banking system. In the calculation of a bank's eligible liabilities funds held on deposit with other banks and holdings of other banks' CDs can be deducted from the gross total of eligible categories of liabilities; they are therefore often referred to as 'deductibles'.

(4) A bank's net deposit liability in sterling to its overseas offices.* Banks that operate both in the UK and abroad receive sterling funds from overseas offices and place sterling funds with those offices. The excess of the total of sums received over the total of sums placed constitutes resources usable in the United Kingdom and therefore, clearly, must be within the ambit of control just as any other sterling resources so usable. Although sterling deposits placed with overseas offices can be set against sterling deposits taken from them, the excess of sterling claims on over liabilities to overseas offices is not deductible from eligible liabilities because it represents a use of sterling resources and not a reduction of the available volume of these resources. An overseas office of a UK bank is defined as: head office, parent company, branch, or wholly owned subsidiary of the bank itself or its parent company.

(5) A bank's net liability in foreign currencies (including currencies of sterling area countries outside the UK). UK banks operate in many foreign currencies as well as in sterling. Generally they tend to match foreign currency liabilities by foreign currency assets, but such matching is seldom precise. An excess of foreign currency liabilities over foreign currency assets indicates that some foreign currency funds have been switched into sterling, thus supplementing sterling resources. Thus, the foreign currency counterpart of these sterling resources is included in eligible liabilities. An excess of foreign currency assets over foreign currency liabilities (switching of sterling into foreign currencies) is not deductible from eligible liabilities because it represents a use of sterling resources and not a reduction in their volume.

(6) The amount of eligible liabilities obtained by adding together the categories (1) to (5) is then adjusted by subtracting 60 per cent of the net value of transit items in each bank's balance sheet. Net value of transit items is defined as cheques drawn on and in course of collection from other banks and all debit items in transit between

* Northern Ireland banks may exclude net liabilities to their offices in the Republic of Ireland.

a bank's own branches, *less* credits in the course of transmission to other banks and between a bank's own branches. Adjustment for transit items is needed to avoid double-counting of some items and leaving others out of account. The figure of 60 per cent of net transit items has been agreed between the banks and the authorities as representing, approximately, the effect of transit items on deposits and, consequently, on eligible liabilities. If credit transit items exceed debit items, so that the net value is negative, the 60 per cent of the net figure is added to a bank's eligible liabilities.

Eligible liabilities represent, for each bank and for the banking system as a whole, the total of short-term sterling resources available for lending. Thus they constitute a very important monetary aggregate, and it is by influencing its magnitude – by forcing the banks to reduce, or by inducing them to expand, eligible liabilities – that the authorities can regulate the magnitude of current expansion of bank credit. Needless to say, customers' deposits are the principal component of eligible liabilities.

Eligible reserve assets comprise the following asset categories (cf. *Bank of England Quarterly Bulletin*, December 1971, p. 485).

(1) Balances with the Bank of England (except special deposits and supplementary special deposits). London clearing banks are required to maintain at the head office of the Bank balances amounting to $1\frac{1}{2}$ per cent of their eligible liabilities.[3] These banks must, of course, hold balances with the Bank of England to meet claims on them arising out of the clearing of cheques, etc. But the maintenance of regular balances by London clearing banks is important for the Bank of England and facilitates its operations in the market. Other banks are not required to hold balances with the Bank of England, and in fact their balances with the Bank are negligible in amount. Notes and coin held in the banks' tills and Bank of England notes held as cover for their own note issues do not count as eligible reserve assets.
(2) British government Treasury bills and Treasury bills of the Northern Ireland government.
(3) Money at call with the London money market. The London money market is defined as comprising: members of the London Discount Market Association (discount houses), discount brokers and money trading departments of certain banks, money brokers and

jobbers operating in the gilt edged market. All loans must be at call or callable and must be secured.

(4) British government stocks and government guaranteed nationalized industries' stocks with one year or less to final maturity.
(5) Local authority bills eligible for rediscount at the Bank of England. To be eligible for rediscount at the Bank local authority bills must have the original currency of less than six months and must meet certain other requirements.
(6) Commercial bills eligible for rediscount at the Bank of England (up to a maximum of 2 per cent of eligible liabilities). The principal condition for eligibility for rediscount is that bills must be accepted by certain British or Commonwealth banks (accepting houses, London and Scottish clearing banks, some British overseas banks, Commonwealth banks that have long had branches in London and some other banks). The restriction of bill holdings as reserves to 2 per cent of eligible liabilities is due to the need to limit the use of private sector debt in the reserve base of the banking system. Otherwise the banks might be able to use one type of lending to the private sector to provide themselves with means to expand other types of private sector loans – great over-expansion of bank credit might thus result.[4]

All eligible reserve assets are high-quality, liquid assets; their holdings can be adjusted easily by operations in the market and, if necessary, they can be shifted on to the Bank of England – indirectly in the case of money at call.

Money at call, mostly placed with the discount houses, is quantitatively the most important of reserve assets. This raises an important issue. Discount houses use funds placed with them to acquire assets that are partly public sector debt and partly private sector debt. To the extent that an increase in the banks' placements of money at call is used by discount houses to lend to the private sector, the banking system experiences an equal increase in eligible liabilities (deposits) and in eligible reserve assets, i.e. a strengthening of the reserve position which makes possible expansion of bank lending. To lessen the extent of such developments some restrictions have had to be imposed on the freedom of discount houses to lend to the private sector.

The arrangement agreed between the Bank of England and the

London Discount Market Association in 1971 (which discount brokers, money brokers and money trading departments of certain banks also accepted) was that they would keep at least 50 per cent of borrowed funds in specified categories of public sector debt. Borrowed funds were defined to include sterling loans obtained from all sources *less* sterling lending to other discount houses, discount and money brokers and money trading departments of banks *plus* the excess of foreign currency liabilities over foreign currency assets. Specified categories of public sector debt were listed as follows (*Bank of England Quarterly Bulletin*, December 1971, p. 487):

(1) UK and Northern Ireland Treasury bills
(2) local authority bills eligible for rediscount at the Bank of England and local authority negotiable bonds
(3) public sector bills guaranteed by the government
(4) company tax reserve certificates (later phased out)
(5) British government and government-guaranteed nationalized industries' stocks with not more than five years to final maturity
(6) local authority stocks with not more than five years to final maturity.

At the same time the Discount Market Association agreed to continue their practice of tendering each week for the entire amount of Treasury bills offered. But tendering at an agreed (syndicated) price was discontinued, each house being free to tender at the price or prices of its own choice. The Bank of England on its part agreed to continue to act as lender of last resort only to members of the discount market.

The operation of the 50 per cent public sector debt ratio rule proved very unsatisfactory, causing disadvantageous and disruptive effects.[5] The old rule was therefore replaced, in July 1973, by the requirement that each discount house's holdings of 'undefined assets' (i.e. assets other than the specified categories of public sector debt[6]) must not exceed the amount equal to 20 times its capital and reserves.[7] The Bank of England emphasized that the 'multiple of 20' was to be treated as 'a maximum not a norm' and repeated its previous injunction that discount houses must maintain 'an appropriate' relation between the total size of each house's business and its capital and reserves.

Special Deposits

All banks (except Northern Ireland banks) and finance houses must place special deposits with the Bank of England when the Bank calls for these deposits. Special deposits are normally called at a uniform percentage rate – normally in relation to each institution's total eligible liabilities, but the authorities have reserved the right to call special deposits from finance houses at a higher rate than from the banks.[8] The authorities have also reserved the right to relate special deposits to some categories of eligible liabilities or to call for them at different rates in relation to different categories of eligible liabilities. Special deposits bear interest at the current Treasury bill rate and their amounts are adjusted monthly to reflect changes in eligible liabilities.

The purpose of special deposits is to impose pressure on the banks' reserve position by forcing them to dispose of eligible reserve assets. Special deposits must be made in cash. The banks and discount houses hold very little cash over and above the amount indispensable for the transaction of current business; cash needed for special deposits must be obtained from the Bank of England. In other words, in order to comply with the call for special deposits the banks must withdraw money at call from the discount market and reduce purchases of bills from the market – forcing discount houses to sell bills to, and to obtain advances from, the Bank of England – and to sell Treasury and local authority bills to the Bank's agent in the money market or government stocks to the government broker in the gilt-edged market.[9] The effect of these operations on the balance sheets of the banks is to reduce holdings of eligible reserve assets (this reduction being balanced on the assets side by an equal increase in special deposits) while leaving eligible liabilities unchanged. More important, however, is the effect that the operations connected with the placement of special deposits have on interest rates: short-term interest rates and gilt-edged rates at the short end tend to rise; there also occur changes in the structure of interest rates. The shaprness of the rise in interest rates depends to a large extent on the policy of the Bank of England: on the terms (penal) it imposes on last resort assistance, and on the proportion of assistance given at current market rates rather than on penal terms. The rise in the level of interest rates and changes to the structure of rates are very important. They affect the public's demand for assets, attracting it towards financial assets which the banks are willing to sell. They also induce the banks to raise their base rates and to adjust appropriately deposit and lending rates related to base rates. Higher interest charges encourage debtors to reduce their indebtedness to the banks whenever possible and discourage prospective borrowers from borrowing. It is the rise in interest rates that makes it possible for the banks to dispose of non-reserve assets, the fall in assets being balanced by an equal reduction in eligible liabilities (deposits).

Supplementary Special Deposits

The supplementary special deposits scheme – known in the city jargon as 'the corset' – was introduced in December 1973 for a limited period in order to restrain the banks from excessive bidding for funds. The authorities considered that aggressive competition among banks for deposits, which developed in 1972–73, caused an undue rise in short-term interest rates, induced severe distortions in the structure of rates and made possible excessive expansion of lending to the private sector and, consequently, excessive monetary expansion generally. The scheme was re-introduced in November 1976 and again in June 1978.

When the scheme is in operation, supplementary special deposits on which no interest is payable must be lodged with the Bank of England by any bank[10] or finance house whose interest-bearing eligible liabilities (IBELs)[11] exceed the officially determined 'permitted' or 'penalty-free' level.

The authorities determine the 'permitted' level of IBELs by applying a percentage figure of their own choosing to the base level of IBELs which is the average of these liabilities outstanding at the reporting dates during a specified period preceding the activation of the scheme. The banks and finance houses are allowed an adjustment period of six months to bring the actual level of IBELs[12] to or below the 'permitted' level. If the scheme remains in operation after the adjustment period (as has so far always been the case), the permitted level of IBELs is increased every month by a constant percentage of the base level. Thus, when the supplementary special deposits scheme is operative the authorities specify the 'permitted' growth of IBELs of individual banks and finance houses.

When the scheme was first introduced in December 1973 the base level of IBELs was the average of the amounts outstanding in October, November and December 1973 and the permitted level of IBELs for June 1974 (at the end of the adjustment period) was 108 per cent of the base level, subsequently increasing by $1\frac{1}{2}$ per cent of the base level per month.

A bank or finance house whose actual level of IBELs exceeds the permitted level is required to place a fraction of the excess with the Bank of England as a supplementary special deposit. The size of that fraction (or the rate of supplementary special deposits) depends on the size of the excess: an excess not greater than 3 per cent of the base level of IBELs attracts supplementary special deposits at the rate of 5 per cent; an excess greater than 3 per cent but not greater than 5 per cent of the base figures attracts them at the rate of 25 per cent; an excess of IBELs greater than 5 per cent of the base level imposes on the institution concerned the obligation to place supplementary special deposits at the rate of 50 per cent[13]

The purpose of supplementary special deposits is to discourage banks from increasing their loanable resources by bidding for funds (i.e. offering 'high' interest rates) in the money market. The discouragement is generated because the need to place a fraction of funds so obtained as a non-interest-bearing special deposit (in addition to having to use $12\frac{1}{2}$ per cent of these funds to hold reserve assets) raises the cost of genuinely loanable funds considerably, thus making their profitable employment in loans satisfying the criteria of prudent banking virtually impossible.

The Expected Operation of the Competition and Credit Control System

In designing the competition and credit control scheme its authors intended to provide the authorities with the means of exercising firm control over the movements of the principal monetary aggregates: the stock of money, domestic credit expansion (DCE), total volume of bank and finance house credit, etc. Responses of these aggregates to measures of monetary policy, e.g. open market operations or special deposits, are always indirect and are brought about by the working of an adjustment mechanism. The authors of the scheme envisaged the following adjustment mechanism.[14]

(1) Given the acceptance by the banks and finance houses of the obligation to maintain agreed minimum reserve ratios, the power to call for special deposits enables the authorities to impose pressure

on the reserve position of the banks (and finance houses), i.e. to reduce their holdings of eligible reserve assets, so as to make the margin between the actual and the required (minimum) reserve ratios uncomfortably narrow.

(2) Official action itself and the responses of banks and finance houses and of the discount houses to the pressure imposed by the authorities – disposals of non-reserve assets and/or decreases in purchases of assets – cause an upward pressure on a wide range of market interest rates and thus on bank lending rates.

(3) Changes in interest rates causing changes in relative rates of return give rise to adjustments in asset portfolios of the banks and of the public, some of these adjustments consisting of asset substitutions and some reflecting changes in liabilities of the public and of the banks respectively.

The crucial feature of this mechanism[15] is the fundamental importance of changes in interest rates. The immediate reaction of banks to reserve pressure, i.e. action to dispose of non-reserve assets by appropriate operations in parallel money markets and in the gilt-edged market, cannot be expected to result in a substantial contraction in the volume of bank deposits. These operations are, however, very important because they cause the relevant interest rates to rise. The banks determine their base rates (to which lending rates are closely related) by reference to interest rates ruling in financial markets, and thus the rise in interest rates extends promptly to rates directly relevant to bank lending to industrial, commercial and personal borrowers.

The significance of the rise in the banks' lending rates lies in their effects on the demand for bank advances. Unless the demand is considered to be perfectly inelastic with respect to the rate of interest, a rise in lending rates must reduce it. Just before the introduction of the competition and credit control system, the then Governor of the Bank of England asserted the willingness of the authorities to put such pressure on bank lending rates as necessary to ensure that the demand for bank loans is reduced to conform to official monetary targets. A decrease in the demand for bank credit reveals itself partly in a fall in the rate at which overdrafts authorized by the banks are utilized and other types of loans are committed and partly in a rise in the rate at which outstanding overdrafts are liquidated and other loans repaid. These two tendencies combine to cause a decrease in net lending, and, if the pressure is strong enough and maintained long enough, net lending may become negative. The banks can strengthen and accelerate the process by stiffening criteria of creditworthiness and other conditions (other than the rate of interest) on which they grant loans; to the extent that unsuccessful applicants for advances would have *used* their overdrafts, etc., the rate of new lending is further reduced in relation to what it would have been if the banks had been able to maintain a less restrictive attitude.

If the object of official policy is to reduce the stock of money, net lending by the banks must become negative and must remain negative until the amount of bank advances outstanding has been appropriately reduced. It should be observed that the bulk of the reduction in the volume of deposits corresponding to decreases in the banks' holdings of assets must be the counterpart of the reduction in the total of advances. This is so because, clearly, the banks do not reduce their holdings of reserve assets, and their operations in parallel money markets and in the gilt-edged market cannot be expected to cause substantial changes in bank deposits (see pp. 77 and 81–2 for a fuller discussion of this problem). Advances are the only asset category large enough to absorb the necessary adjustment.

The fact that the bulk of the decrease in the volume of bank deposits (and therefore in the stock of money) must be the counterpart of the fall in the total of advances, and the fact that the fall in advances is seen as the result of the damping-down effect of the rise in interest rates on the demand for bank loans, taken together have very important implications.

Net repayment of bank advances indicates that some economic activities in the private sector which were or would be profitable at a lower level of interest rates are no longer considered attractive at the higher level to which interest rates have been pushed by official action and market pressures. In other words, it indicates that spending decisions have been revised so as to reduce outlays on goods and services, causing a fall in the flow of aggregate demand. This means that the flow of funds from the private sector to the banks (net repayment of advances) represents the release by the private sector of funds that cannot be profitably used, and it follows from this that the decrease in the stock of money that is the counterpart of the net repayment of bank loans is a consequence of the private sector's decisions to reduce spending not their cause.[16] Several interesting issues arising in this connection will be considered in chapter 6.

CHAPTER FOUR

Creation of Reserves within the Banking Sector

The object of a monetary control system is to enable the authorities to influence the activities of the banks and therefore the volume of monetary aggregates generated by these activities. This influence can be effectively exercised if the authorities are able to affect the reserve position of the banks – to tighten it if they wish to impose a measure of restraint on the banks and to make it easier if they wish to encourage the banks to expand.

Under competition and credit control arrangements special deposits are the principal instrument for influencing the reserve position of the banks: by calling for special deposits the authorities can tighten the banks' reserve position, and by releasing special deposits previously placed by the banks they can ease it. At first sight special deposits appear to be a very effective instrument for controlling bank reserves. To meet calls for special deposits the banks must dispose of reserve assets to obtain the necessary cash – the authorities would not supply cash in exchange for other assets. Thus, by means of special deposits the authorities can reduce the banks' holdings of reserve assets so as to make them too low to support expansion of eligible liabilities or even to maintain their current level. It appears that special deposits are an effective instrument for putting the banks under reserve pressure; in fact, the position is more complicated.

Reserve pressure is effective (in the sense of making it impossible for the banks to expand or forcing them to undertake operations designed to bring about a contraction of eligible liabilities) only if the banks cannot replenish their holdings of reserve assets by buying them from non-bank holders, or by creating them by operations within the banking sector. Clearly, if the banks can quickly replenish their reserves there is no need for them to take steps to reduce eligible liabilities, and official attempts to impose such a reduction are frustrated.

Reserve-creating Operations

Treasury bills, gilt-edged securities within a year of maturity, local authority bills and, of course, commercial bills are held by economic units outside the banking sector. In principle there is nothing to prevent the banks from buying them from holders, giving them deposits in payment. The result of such operations is an equal increase in deposits and reserves so that the reserve ratio rises; if these operations are carried out when bank reserves are under pressure their result is to ease this pressure. In practice the banks are very unlikely to be able to achieve quickly a significant increase in reserves by buying eligible reserve assets from outside holders. Non-bank holdings are not very large and are scattered so that their acquisition in substantial amounts is bound to be difficult and costly.[1] These operations cannot, strictly speaking, be described as reserve-*creating*: their object is to draw into the banking system existing eligible reserve assets held by non-bank economic units.

Similarly, reserves are not *created*, in the strict sense of the term, in the case of arranged transfers of eligible reserve assets from discount houses to the banks. These transactions, broadly similar in nature to those outlined above, are much more important, because discount houses hold large amounts of reserve assets and large-scale transactions between the banks and discount houses can easily be arranged.

The simplest of these operations is an asset swap between a bank and a discount house, the former supplying government securities with more than one year but less than five years to final maturity (which do not rank as a reserve asset for the banks but are a 'defined asset' for the discount houses) and the latter providing assets that rank as reserve assets – e.g. Treasury bills or government stocks within one year of maturity – in exchange.

Eligible liabilities of the bank in question remain unchanged but its reserves rise. By swapping assets with a discount house as described above a bank can obviate the need to contract if it had suffered an outflow of reserves, or it can put itself in a position to expand if its reserve ratio was adequate before the operation. In the last mentioned case the bank in question makes new loans. These give rise to claims on it (cheques drawn by the borrowers and deposited by the payees with their own banks) which it meets by surrendering reserve assets to other banks – those presenting claims.[2] In the final position the 'first bank's' eligible liabilities and its total reserves are respectively the same as they were originally; the total of non-reserve assets is also the same, but their composition is different – holdings of gilt-edged securities are smaller and higher-yielding advances larger. From the point of view of the 'first bank' the outcome is as if it sold securities and used the proceeds to make new loans. But from the point of view of the banking system the position is significantly different. On presenting claims on the 'first bank' other banks have acquired from it (or from the clearing bank acting on its behalf) eligible reserve assets, thus experiencing an equal rise in their reserves and eligible liabilities. They are now in a position to make new loans – a process of multiple creation of bank credit (and deposits) takes place. A mere asset swap involving £100,000 Treasury bills may give rise to an increase in the banking system's assets and eligible liabilities (deposits) of up to £800,000 depending on the total magnitude of leakages of reserves during the credit multiplier process.

Operations that are truly reserve-creating – in the sense that they generate reserve assets that previously did not exist at all – almost invariably involve additional placements of money at call with discount houses and other discount market institutions. Such additional placements of call money increase reserves of the banking system, provided that discount houses do not use these funds to make payments to the authorities.

Banks can create reserves by requiring discount houses to repay maturing non-reserve loans while making new loans to them in the form of secured money at call (which is a reserve asset). Other reserve-creating operations are more complicated, and they are therefore explained in detail and illustrated by numerical examples. Banks are assumed to act independently, without collusion; in particular, action to increase reserves is undertaken (and successfully carried out) by one bank only, other banks merely responding in the normal manner to changes in their position resulting from the initiating bank's action. The examples trace the effects of a specified initial transaction throughout the banking system; other transactions are disregarded. Owing to technical differences, transaction sequences (though not the final outcomes) differ slightly according to whether the initiating bank is a clearing bank (examples 1 and 3) or a non-clearing bank (examples 2 and 4).

EXAMPLE 1 *Simplified Balance Sheet of Bank A*

	Eligible liabilities		Assets		
	Deposits	CDs	Reserve assets	Advances	Other assets
1	10,000	1,000	1,375	6,000	3,625
2	10,000	1,100	1,475	6,000	3,625
3	10,000	1,100	1,387·5	6,087·5	3,625
	Initial impact on the balance sheet of Bank B				
4	+87·5		+87·5		
	Final effects on the banking system as a whole (assuming that all banks maintain the reserve ratio as 12·5% and that there are no leakages during the multiplier process, i.e. maximum effects)				
5	+700	+100	+100	+700	0

Suppose that a clearing bank, Bank A, is in balance sheet equilibrium (reserve ratio of 12½ per cent) as shown in line 1 of example 1. It has an opportunity to make an attractive loan but (a) does not have free resources and (b) knows that claims on it which lending will generate will cause a drain of reserve assets. To put itself in a position to make a new loan Bank A issues certificates of deposit to a discount house, at the same time making a call loan to that house to enable it to pay for the CDs. Bank A's balance sheet (line 2) now shows an excess of reserves. The bank makes a new loan, thus enabling the borrower to make payments; these payments give rise to claims on Bank A which it meets by surrendering reserve assets.[3, 4] This is shown in line 3, and it should be observed that Bank A is again in equilibrium.

Reserve assets surrendered by Bank A pass to other banks, in the example Bank B (the rest of the banking system), and are balanced by an equal increase in Bank B's deposits – deposits made by those who had received payments from 'the borrower' (cheques drawn on Bank A) – line 4. Bank B is now in a position to make new loans. An ordinary process of multiple creation of bank credit takes place, and the final outcome of this process, in terms of changes in the combined balance sheet of the whole banking system, is shown in line 5 of the example.

It should be noted that new reserves created by the original transaction between Bank A and a discount house move from Bank A to other banks but always remain within the banking system, so that there has occurred a 'permanent' increase in the reserve base of the system by the full amount of the creation of reserves. The last point, however, reflects the assumption that there is no leakage of reserves during the credit multiplier process. In fact, important leakages are likely to occur; for example, if recipients of payments made by those who have borrowed from banks use their receipts to buy securities from the authorities or foreign currencies from the Exchange Equalization Account, reserves flow out of the banking system; they also flow out if currency is drawn out of the clearing banks and its replacement forces these banks to reduce their balances with the Bank of England.

It should also be noted that it is highly unlikely that only one bank should engage in reserve-creating operations, the rest of the system being passive in this respect though able and willing to expand lending when their deposits and reserves increase. Conditions that tend to induce attempts to create reserves – generally speaking, the existence of greater demand for advances than the banks can meet given their original reserve base – are practically certain to affect most, if not all, banks at the same time. Thus, all banks are likely to be issuing CDs to discount houses and lending to them at the same time – discount houses using money at call placed by some banks to buy certificates of deposits from others and vice versa. The attraction of these operations to discount houses lies in relatively high yield that the banks must allow them on newly issued CDs. Their attraction to the banks lies, of course, in the expansion of advances (the banks' most profitable assets), which they are expected to make possible.

In the foregoing discussion no mention was made of operations of discount houses, other than their initial purchase of CDs, implying that, having bought CDs, the houses hold them. This need not be so. Discount houses are dealers in CDs – they buy them in order to sell them – but unless they use the proceeds to make payments to the authorities their sales of CDs do not affect the totals of bank deposits and of reserve assets in the system, though they do affect their distribution among banks.

Continuing the framework of example 1, suppose that the discount house concerned sells Bank A's CDs to a customer (depositor) of Bank C; i.e., the ownership of a deposit with Bank C passes from the buyer of CDs to the discount house. The discount house now buys commercial bills or other assets from private sector sellers and pays for these assets by drawing on the deposit with Bank C. Assuming, for simplicity, that asset sellers bank with Bank C, the discount house's deposit is now transferred to them. Asset sellers make payments to their own creditors who deposit cheques on Bank C with their own banks, Banks D, E and F, and these banks present claims on Bank C to it and obtain reserve assets in settlement. Thus, Bank C suffers a fall in deposits balanced by an equal decrease in holdings of reserve assets, while deposits and reserves of Banks D, E and F increase by matching total amounts. Expansion by the latter also matches contraction by the former.

Suppose now that the initiating bank is a non-clearing bank, Bank H in example 2, which finds itself in the same position as Bank A in example 1 and reacts to it similarly, i.e. issues CDs to a discount house simultaneously placing additional money at call with it. Line 1 in example 2 shows the original balance sheet[5] of Bank H and line 2 its balance sheet after the issue of CDs. Bank H now makes a loan; it does so by transferring to the borrower a deposit (Bank H's working balance) with Bank K, a clearing bank (line 3). The borrower uses the loan to make payments, and the payees' banks (Bank L representing the rest of the banking system) acquire new deposits and claims on Bank K which when presented are settled by a transfer of balances with the Bank of England from Bank K to Bank L (lines 3a and 3b). It must be observed that at this stage Bank L has a surplus of reserves but Bank K has a reserve deficiency of the same amount. Taken together, Banks K and L cannot expand unless and until reserves of Bank K are increased.[6]

This adjustment can be made and the banks concerned have the incentive to make it. Bank H has a surplus of reserve assets, but its balances with other banks (working balance with Bank K) have gone down (line 3): surplus reserve assets can be used to rebuild its working balance. It can do it in several ways: it can withdraw money at call from the discount market or sell Treasury bills, etc., to discount houses. The

EXAMPLE 2 *Simplified Balance Sheet of Bank H*

	Eligible liabilities			Assets			
	Deposits (non-bank)	Deposits of other banks	Certif. of deposit	Reserve assets	Balances with other banks [a]	Advances	Other assets
1	10,250	–	1,000	1,375	250	6,000	3,625
2	10,250	–	1,100	1,475	250	6,000	3,625
3	10,250	–	1,100	1,475	162·5	6,087·5	3,625
4	10,250	–	1,100	1,387·5	250	6,087·5	3,625
	Impact on the balance sheet of Bank K						
3a	–	−87·5	–	−87·5	–	–	–
4a	–	+87·5	–	+87·5	–	–	–
	Impact on the balance sheet of Bank L						
3b	+87·5	–	–	+87·5			
4b	–	–	–	−87·5 (Bal with B. of England)			
				+87·5 (Money at call)			
	Final effects on the banking system as a whole (assumption as in example 1)						
5	+700	0	+100	+100	0	+700	0

[a] Balances with other banks are deductible in the calculation of eligible liabilities.

houses have the means to repay money at call or to buy bills because, at the same time, Bank L increases placements of call money in order to substitute earning reserve assets for a barren balance with the Bank of England – which it has acquired as a counterpart of the rise in deposits (line 3b). Claims on Bank L are passed by the discount houses to Bank H, which deposits them with Bank K, enabling it to obtain balances with the Bank of England from Bank L (lines 4, 4a and 4b). Alternatively, Bank H can sell Treasury bills directly to Bank K, the latter paying for the bills by crediting Bank H's deposit, or Bank H can sell bills to Bank L and deposit the receipts (in the form of a balance with the Bank of England) with Bank K. When these adjustments have been made the standard process of multiple creation of credit can take place, the final outcome of which is shown in line 5.

It is now necessary to consider whether or not a single bank acting independently can increase its reserves by 'simply placing' additional call money with a discount house, balancing this increase in assets by creating an ordinary sight deposit in favour of the discount house. The answer appears to be that by taking such action a single bank can achieve only a very temporary increase in reserves and that if, in view of the rise in reserves, it increases advances the outcome of these operations will make its reserves deficient. Although a single bank cannot effectively increase its reserves (indeed, tends to lose them), the effects of that bank's actions cause an increase in the reserve base of the rest of the banking system. This makes it possible for the bank that initially attempted to create reserves to restore its holdings of reserve assets or to increase them relatively to their original level. It can do so by selling assets to other banks or to their customers, or by borrowing in the interbank market. Example 3 illustrates the problem.

A clearing bank, Bank X, the balance sheet of which is shown in line 1 of the example, wishes to make a new loan and in order to provide itself with resources for it decides to place an additional amount of money at call with a discount house. To this end it creates a deposit in favour of that discount house and its balance sheet takes the form shown in line 2. Bank X now makes the new loan and meets claims resulting from it by surrendering reserve assets to those presenting claims, viz. Bank Y, representing the rest of the banking system (line 3). At the same time, however, Bank X is faced with another set of claims, namely those due to the use by the discount house in question of the deposit placed at its disposal by Bank X – the discount house draws on that deposit to make payments to the customers (assumed to be economic units in the private sector) who deposit cheques with their banks (Bank Y in the example), and these, in turn, present them to Bank X for settlement (line 4). Bank X now has a reserve deficiency; in the example the deficiency amounts to 87·5.

Reserve assets that have flowed out of Bank X (in the example 187·5, the difference between reserve assets in lines 2 and 4) have shifted to Bank Y, creating an equal amount of deposits with that bank (line 5).

Bank X can restore equilibrium in its balance sheet by selling 'other assets' to Bank Y or to the customers of Bank Y, thus re-establishing balance sheet equilibrium as shown in line 6a. (If Bank Y itself buys

EXAMPLE 3 *Simplified Balance Sheet of Bank X*

	Eligible liabilities		Assets		
	Deposits	Deposits of other banks	Reserve assets	Advances	Other assets
1	10,000	–	1,250	5,000	3,750
2	10,100	–	1,350	5,000	3,750
3	10,100	–	1,262·5	5,087·5	3,750
4	10,000	–	1,162·5	5,087·5	3,750
	Initial impact on the balance sheet of Bank Y				
5	+187·5		+187·5		
	Restoration of equilibrium in the balance sheet of Bank X				
6a	10,000	–	1,250	5,087·5	3,662·5
6b	10,000	100	1,262·5	5,087·5	3,750
	Final effects on the banking system as a whole (assumptions as in example 1)				
7a*i*	+800	–	+100	+700	0
7a*ii*	+800	–	+100	+787·5	−87·5
7b*i*	+800	0	+100	+700	0
7b*ii*	+800	+100	+100	+700	+100

assets from Bank X its reserve assets fall by 87·5 and its 'other assets' increase by the same amount; if customers of Bank Y are the buyers, deposits with Bank Y and its reserve assets decline by 87·5.) Alternatively, Bank X may borrow in the interbank market, but since an increase in interbank indebtedness is an increase in eligible liabilities the loan must provide for the existing reserve deficiency and for the support of the rise in eligible liabilities, (line 6b).

Total holdings of reserve assets by the banking system as a whole are now greater than they were in the original position by the amount of their creation by Bank X. Deposits are also higher, but there is nevertheless a reserve surplus and a process of multiple creation of credit develops. It differs slightly according to the method used by Bank X to restore its balance sheet equilibrium, and the final outcomes are shown in lines 7a*i* if Bank X sells 'other assets' to Bank Y, 7a*ii* if it sells 'other assets' to the customers of Bank Y, and 7b, *i* and *ii* if it obtains an interbank loan from Bank Y. Line 7b*i* shows *net* results, the interbank deposit taken by Bank X being cancelled in the calculation against the interbank loan made by Bank Y; line 7b*ii* shows *gross* results, including the interbank deposit and the interbank loan (under the heading of 'other assets').

As in the case involving the issue of CDs previously discussed, it is highly unlikely that only one bank should attempt to increase reserves, the others remaining passive in this respect. Conditions likely to give rise to attempts to create reserves are likely to be general, affecting all banks. It should be noted that, if all banks increase money at call at the same time, none of them need suffer a serious outflow of reserves as a result of the use of these funds by discount houses – adjustment problems are therefore much easier to cope with.

Creation of reserves by means of a placement of additional call money with a discount house can also be initiated by a non-clearing bank. This case is illustrated in example 4. Line 1 shows the initial balance sheet of a non-clearing bank, Bank Q. This bank decides to add to its reserve base by increasing money at call with a discount house. Being a non-clearing bank, it does so by transferring to the house concerned a part of its working balance with Bank R (a clearing bank). This is shown in line 2, and the effect of the use of new funds by the discount house on the balance sheet of Bank R appears in line 2a. Bank Q makes a loan of the maximum amount possible, given the reserve position that it plans to establish by subsequent adjustments. As the borrower uses the loan Bank Q's working balance with Bank R decreases and Bank R suffers an outflow of reserve assets (balances with the Bank of England) – lines 3 and 3a. Reserves that flow out of Bank R pass to Bank S (representing the rest of the banking system), where they are balanced by equal increases in deposits – lines 2a, 2b, 3a, and 3b. Bank Q must rebuild its working balance by means of one of the operations explained in connection with example 2, and the effects of this action are shown in lines 4, 4a and 4b. These adjustments put the banking system in a position to expand lending, and the final effects are shown in line 5.

Banks can increase their reserves ('create' reserves would not be an accurate description in this case) by discounting eligible commercial bills for loan-seeking customers instead of giving them advances. A single bank must, of course, expect to suffer an outflow of reserve assets

EXAMPLE 4 *Simplified Balance sheet of Bank Q*

	Eligible liabilities		Assets			
	Deposits (non-bank)	Deposits of other banks	Reserve assets	Balances with other banks[a]	Advances	Other assets
1	10,000	–	1,250	250	5,000	3,500
2	10,000	–	1,350	150	5,000	3,500
3	10,000	–	1,350	62·5	5,087·5	3,500
4	10,000	–	1,262·5	150	5,087·5	3,500
	Impact on the balance sheet of Bank R					
2a		–100	–100			
3a		– 87·5	– 87·5			
4a		+ 87·5	+ 87·5			
	Impact on the balance sheet of Bank S					
2b	+100		+100			
3b	+ 87·5		+ 87·5			
4b			– 87·5 (Bal. with B. of England) + 87·5 (Money at call)			
	Final effects on the banking system as a whole (assumption as in example 1)					
5	+700[b] (+100)[c]		+100	–100	+700	0

[a] Deductible in the calculation of eligible liabilities

[b] Deposits of non-bank customers and of other banks

[c] Increase in eligible liabilities due to a decrease in deductibles (balances with other banks) of Bank Q.

as customers who obtained deposits in exchange for bills draw on them to make payments. Thus, that bank cannot increase advances as well as bills discounted. But the banking system experiences a rise in the reserve base equal to the increase in deposits, and this makes possible a general expansion of bank lending. Moreover, if all banks increase the volume of bills discounted none of them need suffer serious outflows of reserves.

The scope for this type of reserve-increasing action is, however, limited. Commercial bills are eligible reserve assets to a maximum of 2 per cent of eligible liabilities, and although actual holdings of eligible bills tend to be significantly below the permitted maximum, the margin is seldom wide. Moreover, the Bank of England keeps a very watchful eye on the volume of acceptance business undertaken by accepting houses and by other banks whose acceptance makes a bill eligible for rediscounting at the Bank of England, and would strongly discourage increases in the volume of acceptances if these increases reflected the desire of banks to increase their holdings of bills ranking as reserve assets. The disapproval of the Bank of England is also likely to restrain the banks from increasing acceptances in order to increase the supply of bills to discount houses and thus to make the houses more willing to take additional money at call from the banks. But the force of the Bank's disapproval has not always been fully effective.

The 'Creation of Reserves Problem'

Operations by means of which substantial amounts of reserves can be created within the banking system all involve lending by the banks to discount houses. Thus, the feasibility of these operations depends on the ability and willingness of discount houses to accept additional amounts of money at call offered to them by the banks.

The ability of discount houses to accept additional funds from the banks (or other lenders) is limited by the requirement 'that the size of each house's total business should bear an appropriate relationship to its capital and reserves'.[7] The 'appropriate relationship' has never been specified in quantitative or quantifiable terms, and it is therefore impossible to determine in a given situation how much additional call money discount houses can take. However, published statistics[8] show that between August 1973 and December 1977 the highest reported total assets multiple[9] was 34·5 (in February 1976) and that the multiple of 33 was exceeded in only four (out of 41) months. In the remaining 37 months of the period the total assets multiple was significantly, often very substantially, lower than 33. This suggests that the total assets multiple of 33 may be taken as indicating the maximum to which a discount house total business can be expanded within limits set by the 'appropriate relationship' requirement. It follows that discount houses are normally able to accept the banks' additional placements of money at call in amounts sufficient to raise the banks' holdings of reserve assets by, perhaps, $\frac{1}{2}$–1 per cent of eligible liabilities (the order of magnitude comparable to special deposits).

The overall ability of discount houses to accept additional placements of money at call is not enough for an effective creation of reserves. For this to take place discount houses must also be able to use additional funds to buy assets from private sector holders. Their ability to do so is roughly indicated by the margin between the discount market's actual undefined assets multiple and the maximum permitted multiple i.e. 20.[10] After the introduction of the limit on discount houses' holdings of undefined assets in July 1973 the undefined assets multiple of the discount market rose quickly, reaching 18·8 in January 1974 and 19·1 in March; it remained very close to – in most cases a little above – that figure until the middle of 1975. Clearly, over that period the banks could not effectively create reserves by placing additional money at call with the discount market. After mid-1975 and until the end of 1977 the undefined assets multiple fluctuated between 11·8 and 16·9 – whatever additional placements of money at call discount houses could accept they could use to buy undefined assets. Over that period there was scope for the creation of significant amounts of bank reserves.

If the discount houses are able to accept additional money at call from the banks, and if they can use it to buy assets (mainly undefined assets) from private sector holders, their willingness to do so (in the absence of moral suasion by the authorities) depends on the profitability of these operations to them. That is to say, it depends on the relationship between current interest rates payable on additional money at call and obtainable on assets acquired with that money and on the expectations about changes in the relevant interest rates.

The current level of interest rates on money at call is virtually certain to be lower than the level of yields on commercial bills, certificates of deposits and several other assets that discount houses may wish to buy. Thus, if interest rates are not expected to rise, participation in reserve-creating operations is very likely to be attractive to discount houses and they can be presumed to be willing to take part in these operations by accepting additional money at call offered to them by the banks. Thus, it appears that, if a tightening of the monetary situation – whether owing to official action or to other causes – is not anticipated, the banking system can expand its own reserves without serious difficulty. In other words, if economic conditions favour general expansion, the banking system can, by its own operations, generate additional supplies of credit needed to provide finance to sustain the rising level of economic activity.

The crucial aspect of the problem of creating reserves within the banking system is the question of whether or not the banks can successfully create new reserves to offset an actual or impending depletion of their reserves caused by calls for special deposits. The importance of this issue is obvious: if the banks can effectively create reserves in such a situation, they have the power to frustrate the policy of the authorities.

The announcement of a call for special deposits profoundly affects the monetary situation. In the first place it generates expectations of increases in interest rates. This is so partly because the impending withdrawal of resources from the banking system is unlikely to be fully matched by a decrease in the demand for them, thus making monetary conditions tighter; partly because at the time of the introduction of the competition and credit control system the Governor of the Bank of England made it clear that the authorities intended to use special deposits as an instrument of upward pressure on interest rates (see p. 40 above); and partly because it is known that to supply the banks with the cash needed to place special deposits discount houses must sell assets to, or borrow from, the Bank of England. Second, discount houses expect, indeed know, that in the near future they will have to sell assets to, or borrow from the Bank of England on worse terms than currently obtainable, quite possibly on penal terms.

The expectation of decreases in asset values and the virtual certainty that they will soon have to borrow from the Bank of England on onerous terms are likely to make discount houses unwilling to expand their holdings of assets and, consequently, unwilling to accept additional money at call from the banks. How strongly discount houses are likely to be deterred from increasing borrowing and buying assets depends on the maturity structure of their portfolios: the greater the proportion of assets very close to maturity, the weaker the deterrent effect; on their expectations of subsequent movements of interest rates: if they expect interest rates to fall again shortly they may decide to pay little attention to a temporary fall in the value of their portfolios; and, finally, on the rates of return obtainable on newly purchased assets: the higher these rates, the stronger the desire to buy them notwithstanding general disadvantages of asset-buying when interest rates are expected to rise.

Another influence that tends to make discount houses unwilling to take more money at call is their appreciation of the probable reaction of the authorities. Faced with attempts by the banking system to nullify or weaken the effects of official action, the authorities are likely to take steps to increase the pressure – not out of pique or in retaliation, but in order to ensure that the effectiveness of their policy is not seriously impaired. In particular, the authorities must be expected to act on interest rates so as to make them rise more and faster than would otherwise be the case, such action involving a sharp stiffening of the terms imposed on last resort loans to discount houses.

The authorities are likely to supplement their formal action by some informal moral suasion to influence the behaviour of discount houses.

The factors and forces discussed in the foregoing paragraphs appear likely to be sufficiently strong to make it very difficult for the banks to secure the co-operation of discount houses in reserve-creating operations designed to increase reserves in anticipation of their depletion by special deposits. Consequently, the banks are unlikely to be able to carry out such operations on a substantial scale.

In the foregoing discussion it has been assumed that official action to reduce bank reserves makes the banks desire to undertake operations to create reserves. This may not be the case. The banks' purpose in attempting to create reserves is to obviate the necessity to contract the volume of bank credit or to preserve the ability to expand it. Thus, reserve-creating operations presuppose the present or expected existence of excess demand for bank credit. Increases in interest rates – especially if the authorities are believed to be prepared to see a substantial rise, if necessary – together with the general atmosphere of monetary restraint or stringency may well have a damping down effect on the demand for bank loans. If this happens the banks' desire to increase their reserve base must weaken and may disappear completely.

The problem of reserve creation by the banks after they have placed special deposits is only slightly different from that of reserve creation in preparation for the placement of special deposits. The crucial point concerns, again, expectations about movements of interest rates, and especially about the probable official policy in this field. If the authorities are expected to react to attempts to create reserves by taking steps to raise interest rates (possibly including another call for special deposits), operations to create reserves are unlikely to be successful, even if they remain attractive to the banks. The attitude of the discount houses – their unwillingness to accept additional money at call – is the principal reason for that.

The foregoing discussion brings out the crucial importance of the rate of interest for the problem of creating bank reserves by means of operations within the banking system. If the discount houses are able to accept additional money at call and use it to buy assets from private sector holders, the factor capable of making them unwilling to do so is the expectation that movements in interest rates are likely to make these transactions unprofitable. High or rising interest rates are also a very important factor which, by damping down demand for bank loans, can reduce or eliminate the banks' desire to undertake reserve-creating operations.

The competition and credit control system has been criticized for making it possible for the banking system to increase its own reserve base. Under easy economic and monetary conditions, when real economic expansion is possible and when, therefore, monetary expansion is necessary and desirable, this is indeed so. But under such conditions this feature of the system is an advantage rather than a defect. It enables the banks to provide themselves quickly and easily with such additional reserves as are needed to sustain the expansion in the supply of credit *pari passu* with the rise in the demand for it. The ability of the banking system to create its own reserves has another advantage: it increases the flexibility of the system and enables it to cope satisfactorily with unintended temporary shortages of reserves.

The fact that the banks can create their own reserves is a real defect of the system only if they can do so to obstruct official policy of restraint. Reasons have been given for the view that, if monetary conditions are tight, causing expectations of rising interest rates – and especially if the authorities are known, or are considered likely, to strengthen and promote the upward tendency of interest rates – the banks may find that some types of reserve-creating operations cannot easily be undertaken on a large scale. Nevertheless, even under such conditions, the ability of the authorities to control the reserve position of the banking system is imperfect and uncertain. Consequently, when expansion of bank credit appears attractive to the banks, the authorities may find themselves unable to force the banks to abandon expansionary credit policies.

CHAPTER FIVE

Public Sector Borrowing from the Banking Sector and its Effects on Bank Reserves

Public Sector Borrowing Requirement and its Financing

The public sector borrowing requirement (PSBR) is the amount by which the expenditure of the public sector (including loans and grants to the private and overseas sectors) exceeds its receipts during a period. In other words, it is the amount the public sector must borrow from other sectors during the period in question. Public sector borrowing requirement is a 'net' concept in the sense that it excludes borrowing needed to re-finance maturing debt; thus, *ex post*, it indicates the increase in the amount of public sector debt outstanding.

Miscalculations, forecasting errors, etc., apart, the size of the public sector borrowing requirement is a policy-determined variable: it is the net result of all decisions concerning outlays and receipts of the central government, local authorities and public corporations. The size of the public sector borrowing requirement can be altered only by changing relevant policy decisions. The monetary authorities may urge the government and other bodies in the public sector to make policy changes to alter their total borrowing requirement, but they cannot over-rule the government and other decision-makers. Thus, once the size of the public sector borrowing requirement has been firmly determined, monetary authorities must take it as given and must organize their operations accordingly.

To finance the borrowing requirement the public sector borrows (1) from the UK private sector, (2) in certain circumstances, from the overseas sector, and (3) from the UK banking sector.

Borrowing from the UK private sector, i.e. from domestic non-bank lenders, takes the form of sales (net) of public sector marketable and non-marketable debt to the suppliers of funds. This borrowing represents a direct or indirect transfer of current private sector saving to the public sector. Thus, that part of the current income of the private sector that is not used to finance current private consumption or private investment is made available to finance the excess of the expenditure of the public sector over its receipts.

The phrase 'public sector borrowing from the overseas sector' is used to describe the channelling to the public sector of sterling funds generated by several types of external transactions of the economy. The most important among these sterling funds are those that constitute the counterpart of the total currency flow[1] when this is *negative*, i.e. when the balance of payments is in deficit. To make possible the execution of *net* external payments the Exchange Equalization Account (EEA) supplies the necessary foreign currencies, i.e. sells them, for sterling, to those demanding them. If the foreign currencies are supplied from official reserves, the EEA lends the sterling proceeds of these sales to the Exchequer, thus making them available for the financing of the public sector borrowing requirement. If, in order to avoid depleting official reserves, the authorities obtain foreign currency loans from foreign governments or banks, the Exchequer sells foreign currencies thus acquired to the Exchange Equalization Account, which pays for them with sterling funds obtained from buyers of foreign currencies – again, sterling proceeds of sales of foreign currencies needed to make net external payments are available for the financing of the public sector borrowing requirement.[2]

Certain transactions included in the calculation of the total currency flow themselves constitute supply of loan finance to the public sector. The most obvious and direct among these transactions are loans raised abroad by public sector institutions. Such loans finance directly a fraction of the public sector borrowing requirement, usually one that has a counterpart in foreign currency expenditure of the borrowing public sector bodies. But it must be noted that these foreign currency loans reduce by an equal amount the total negative currency flow and thus the flow of finance from the EEA to the Exchequer.[3] If foreign currency loans are raised to finance sterling expenditure, public sector borrowers sell foreign currencies to the Exchange Equalization Account for sterling; the Exchequer need not provide funds to the public sector borrowers concerned, but the flow of funds to it from the EEA is correspondingly reduced. Similarly, if overseas residents buy public sector debt, whether from debt-issuing bodies in the public sector (the central government, local authorities, etc.) or from domestic holders to the extent that the latter use the proceeds to finance – directly or indirectly – new purchases of public sector debt, foreign lenders provide funds for the financing of the public sector borrowing requirement, but the flow of funds from the Exchange Equalization Account to the Exchequer is reduced by the same amount.

UK banks regularly make foreign currency loans to the public sector. This class of bank lending is made possible by foreign currency deposits placed with UK banks by (in most cases) their non-resident customers. Such loans contribute directly to the financing of public sector borrowing requirement – that fraction of it that corresponds to foreign currency expenditure of the public sector. Whether or not they affect the amount that the Exchange Equalization Account can make available to the Exchequer depends on the use the banks would make of foreign currency deposits in question if they did not provide foreign currency loans to the public sector. If the banks used them to make investments in foreign markets, or to make loans to non-residents, or to lend to residents to finance payments in foreign currencies, the position of the Exchange Equalization Account would be unaffected.[4] But if the banks decided to switch foreign currency resources into sterling, the amount which the Exchange Equalization Account could make available to the Exchequer would be reduced. Foreign currency deposits with UK banks and their use do not have the same monetary significance as domestic sterling deposits and sterling assets balancing them, and for this reason public sector borrowing from the banks in foreign currency is treated as borrowing from the overseas sector and not from the banking sector.

If the supply of funds made available by economic units in the private and overseas sectors is inadequate to finance the public sector borrowing requirement fully, the shortfall must be provided for by borrowing from the banking sector together with increases in notes and coin in circulation with the public.[5]

Public Sector Borrowing from the Banking Sector

The banks and discount houses lend to the public sector – the central government, local authorities, nationalized industries and public corporations – by buying various instruments of debt (Treasury, local authority and other public sector bills, government and local authority bonds and stocks, etc.) and by making loans of several types (temporary loans to local authorities, loans of a similar character to other public sector bodies and ordinary overdrafts and advances). Whatever its form, bank lending to the public sector provides for the financing of the public sector borrowing requirement.

Particular importance attaches to banking sector lending to finance current requirements of the Exchequer, i.e. to provide funds to meet, day by day, Exchequer outlays for which finance from other sources is not available. The principal source of these funds is the flow of payments by discount houses for their *net* acquisitions of Treasury bills.[6] To finance these payments discount houses must increase their borrowing from, or sales of, Treasury bills to the banks. Thus, the problem is the ability of the banks to supply the necessary funds to discount houses, and this problem is largely solved automatically.

Apart from purely internal transactions within the government sector, Exchequer payments give rise to transfers of balances from public deposits to bankers' deposits at the Bank of England. If Exchequer payments are made to non-bank economic units in the private sector or in the public sector, e.g. local authorities, public corporations, etc., the additions to bankers' deposits are the counterpart of increases in bank deposits of the recipients of payments from the Exchequer. If Exchequer payments are made to the banks, e.g. payments to redeem Treasury bills or gilt-edged securities held by the banks on the date of maturity, additions to bankers' deposits balance decreases in the banks' other assets. Exchequer receipts involve symmetrically opposite adjustments: balances are transferred from bankers' deposits to public deposits and the decreases in the former are balanced either by reductions in deposits of non-bank economic units that have made payments to the Exchequer or by increases in the banks' other assets.

It is clear that, if Exchequer payments on a particular day[7] exceed that day's Exchequer receipts (*excluding* receipts from discount houses for net purchases of Treasury bills), there takes place a net transfer from public deposits to bankers' deposits at the Bank of England, approximately equal to the difference between Exchequer receipts and payments. The resulting increase in the banks' balances with the Bank of England constitutes, very largely and sometimes entirely, accumulation of *excess* cash holdings.[8] The banks are normally anxious (for profitability reasons) to dispose of their cash surpluses, and their usual method of accomplishing this is to increase placements of money at call with discount houses or to increase purchases of Treasury bills from them. The discount houses are thus put in funds to pay for the Treasury bills they have contracted to buy (net). In short, under present arrangements an excess of government payments over receipts has the following financial effects.

(1) As the government draws (net) on public deposits at the Bank of England, bankers' deposits increase.
(2) This enables the banks to make additional loans to discount houses and the houses use these funds to pay for their net purchases of Treasury bills.[9]
(3) Payments made by discount houses are credited to Public Deposits and cover the government's net drawings on these accounts.

In an ideal situation the government, the banks and the discount houses would all balance their books as a result of these operations. In practice, residual discrepancies normally tend to arise, mainly because net acquisitions of Treasury bills on particular days are determined in advance (at the weekly tender for Treasury bills) and independently of the relationship between Exchequer receipts and payments taking place on particular days. These discrepancies are eliminated mainly by official market operations in Treasury bills: sales, if the net amount of bills that discount houses have contracted to buy on the day in question is inadequate to provide for the Exchequer needs; purchases, if the opposite is the case.[10]

Public sector (central government) net spending financed by borrowing from the banking sector as just described causes important changes in liabilities and assets of the banking sector. The banks experience an increase in deposits, balanced in the first instance by a rise in their balances with the Bank of England, which is, however, promptly and almost wholly replaced by increases in loans to discount houses (mainly at call but sometimes also loans at short notice) and in holdings of Treasury and other bills bought from discount houses.[11] Discount houses increase their debts to the banks and their holdings of Treasury bills. The Banking Department of the Bank of England experiences a small increase in bankers' deposits and balances it by adding to its holdings of Treasury bills.

In the case of the banks, balance sheet changes just described strengthen their reserve position and therefore increase their ability – and, most probably, willingness – to expand lending (including acquisition of government stocks, placement of funds in parallel markets, etc., as well as overdrafts and advances).[12] From the point of view of monetary control the crucial issue is the magnitude of the expansion of bank lending to the private sector; it is crucial because new lending to the private sector generates new deposits, i.e. causes the stock of money to increase. The magnitude of the expansion of bank lending depends, primarily, on the extent to which the banks, as a group, retain the additional reserves they have acquired.

Reserve assets can flow out of the banking system for several reasons. In the first place the banks may wish to replace some low-yielding reserve assets by higher yielding non-reserve public sector debt, e.g. gilt-edged securities with more than one year to final maturity.[13] Second, the authorities can force the banks to surrender reserve assets by calling for special deposits.[14] Third, action taken by bank customers whose deposits have increased – whether as a result of government net spending or of the expansion of bank lending – tends to cause, gradually, important outflows of reserves from the banks. Three principal cases can be readily identified. There tends to occur an increase in the public's demand for currency. This is due partly to the fact that as aggregate demand grows the volume of payments that are most conveniently made in cash also grows and economic units find it necessary to increase the average amount of notes and coin that they hold. They obtain the additional currency by drawing it from the banks in exchange for deposits.[15] Notes and coin held by the banks are not reserve assets, but their outflow, nevertheless, affects bank reserves. The banks try to keep their holdings of notes and coin as small as possible, but because of this they find it necessary to replenish them immediately, whenever they have become depleted. They do so by drawing on their balances with the Bank of England, which *are* reserve assets.[16] Some bank customers whose deposits have increased may consider that this has unbalanced their portfolios. To correct this they use surplus deposits to buy other assets. If these other assets are gilt-edged securities or other instruments of public sector debt bought directly or indirectly from the authorities their purchases force the banks to surrender reserve assets to the authorities when bank customers' cheques are presented for settlement. Similarly, if new deposits are used to acquire foreign currencies from the Exchange Equalization Account (to pay for net imports) the settlement of the resulting claims causes a decrease in the bank holdings of reserves.

The discussion in the preceding paragraph concerned, in effect, various cases of lending to the public sector (central government) by the banks, by non-bank economic units in the private sector, by the Bank of England and by the EEA. An important feature common to all these transactions should be noted. Although they all constitute lending to the government, they do not generate flows of spendable funds to it; their importance lies in that they enable the government to adjust the structure of its existing debt in several respects (to substitute debt instruments that *are not* eligible reserve assets for instruments that *are* reserve assets; to replace short-term debt by long(er)-term debt; to replace debt to the banks by debt to non-bank economic units, etc.). Thus, the significance of these operations is primarily monetary rather than financial.

The bulk of the expansion of bank lending made possible by additions to bank reserves usually consists of bank lending to the private sector. But various loans to public sector bodies are also made, the most important among them being temporary (market) loans to local authorities and advances to local authorities and nationalized industries. Two points must be noted in connection with these bank loans to the public sector. (1) Assets that the banks acquire are not eligible reserve assets. (2) The making of these loans is technically very different from bank lending to the government previously discussed: clearing banks lend by claims upon themselves, and non-clearing banks by transferring their own claims on the clearing banks to the borrowers. Bank lending to the public sector which exhibits these two characteristics generates a flow of spendable funds to the public sector, but the banking system's holdings of reserve assets remain unchanged (unless the borrowers use the funds so obtained to make payments to the central government). The counterpart of the increase in bank assets is a rise in bank deposits – not, however, of the borrowers themselves (except momentarily in some cases) but of the recipients of the borrowers' payments. It follows from the foregoing that the fact that loans and advances are made by the banks to their public sector and not to private sector customers does not affect the magnitude of the expansion of bank lending or the magnitude of the increase in the volume of deposits.

Temporary loans and advances to local authorities, nationalized industries, etc., have an obvious financial significance. But they also have considerable monetary significance. This arises from the fact that the central government is most unlikely not to provide financial support to a local authority or a public corporation that finds itself unable to raise the funds it needs to honour its commitments. Thus, if local authorities, nationalized industries, etc., fail to finance their borrowing requirements from market sources (including banks), the central government must be assumed to supply the deficiency. To do this the government must increase its own borrowing; this additional borrowing is most likely to be borrowing from the banking sector, causing an increase in the flow of reserve assets to the banks. It follows therefore that, given the total amount that the public sector must borrow from the banking sector, the making by the banks of loans and advances to local authorities and nationalized industries has the effect of reducing the supply of reserve assets to the banks.

The foregoing discussion of public sector borrowing from the banking sector clearly indicates that there are involved several groups of transactions and operations, conceptually quite distinct from one another and having different effects, but closely connected with one another, and in some cases dependent on one another. Published data do not make it possible to identify changes in bank assets and liabilities arising out of the various operations involved. Recorded changes in the balance sheet of the UK banking system show the final outcome of the interaction of all the operations concerned that have taken place in the reporting periods together with the effects of several other influences and pressures at work at the same time. Nevertheless, an analaysis of changes in bank reserves in relation to public sector borrowing from the banking sector yields interesting and important results.

Public Sector Borrowing from the Banking Sector and Changes in Bank Reserves

Public sector borrowing from the banking sector tends to increase bank reserves, and repayment of public sector debt to the banking sector tends to decrease bank reserves. But there are several important influences that affect this relationship.

(1) In lending to the public sector the banks can choose whether to acquire reserve or non-reserve assets.
(2) Money at call placed in the discount market is a reserve asset, whether used by discount market institutions to hold public sector debt or debt issued by private sector institutions – thus, changes in the composition of the discount market's assets can affect the relation between public sector borrowing or repayment of debt and changes in bank reserves.
(3) Banks can increase or decrease reserves by varying credit given by buying commercial bills (subject to the 2 per cent rule).
(4) In co-operation with discount houses the banks can convert non-reserve into reserve assets and vice versa.
(5) In some circumstances the banks (usually in co-operation with discount houses) can create or extinguish their own reserves.

The following hypothesis can be formulated: changes in the banks' holdings of reserves are positively related, without lag, to the volume of public sector borrowing from the banking sector, but the magnitude of the former is considerably smaller than that of the latter. This hypothesis can be tested and the overall relationship between the two variables quantitatively estimated by means of regression analysis.

The equations below show regressions of changes in total reserves of the banks (y) on public sector borrowing from the banking sector (x) obtained by the method of least squares from monthly figures June 1975–December 1977 and January 1978–October 1979 respectively.[17] For the former period the regression equation is:

$y = 0{\cdot}23x + 17{\cdot}36$
Standard error $= 0{\cdot}067$
Coefficient of determination $r^2 = 0{\cdot}212$

and for the latter period (to August 1979):

$y = 0{\cdot}11x + 30{\cdot}42$
Standard error = 0·044
Coefficient of determination $r^2 = 0{\cdot}32$

In both cases the regression coefficients have the right sign (positive) and are smaller than one, and the results are formally significant. Thus, regression analysis can be said to support both parts of the hypothesis stated above. But it must be noted that data for particular months and quarters show considerable deviations from the regression relationships; this means that these equations cannot be used to estimate the effects of month-to-month variations in public sector borrowing from the banking sector on bank reserves. Moreover, the difference between the two equations indicates that in the longer run the overall relationship between the two variables is substantially changeable.

A broad inference that can be drawn from this analysis is that public sector borrowing from the banking sector affects the reserve position of the banks only to a limited extent. In other words, the monetary significance of the recourse of the public sector to borrowing from the banking sector is not as great as might be expected. At the time, when the public sector regularly budgets for large deficits so that public sector borrowing from the banking sector is likely to occur year after year, it is comforting that only a fraction of such borrowing is reflected in increases in the banks' holdings of reserve assets. On the other hand, the conclusion implies that even a substantial reduction in public sector borrowing from the banking sector may not bring about a significant decrease in the growth of bank reserves. It must also be noted that, although regression equations indicate a positive relationship between public sector borrowing from the banking sector and changes in bank reserves in both periods studied, the relationship in particular months of these periods was not infrequently negative. Thus, between June 1975 and the end of 1977 public sector borrowed from the banking sector in 17 months – bank reserves increased in 11 of these months and decreased in 6; public sector repaid debt to the banking sector in 14 months – bank reserves increased in 7 of these and decreased in 7. Between January 1978 and October 1979 public sector borrowing from the banking sector occurred in 12 months and coincided with increases in bank reserves in 10 of them and with decreases in 2; repayment of public sector debt to the banking sector occurred in 10 months – bank reserves increased in 6 of these and decreased in 4.

Examination of the movements of the reserve ratios of the banking system and of the principal groups of banks shows that between June 1975 and October 1979 there were not many instances of sudden, sharp but short-lived changes in these ratios. This suggests that changes in holdings of reserves were broadly in line with the banks' needs and requirements. It appears, therefore, that the banks used lending to the public sector to provide themselves with additional reserve assets if, and approximately to the extent that, they wanted to add to their reserves, but they were usually successful in preventing their lending to the public sector from excessively swelling their reserves. On the other hand, it appears that the banks were able, in most cases, to offset or more than offset reserve losses caused by repayment of public sector debt by means of operations resulting in acquisitions of reserve assets.

It follows from the foregoing that public sector borrowing from the banking sector (a consequence of the public sector borrowing requirement being larger than financeable from non-bank sources) facilitates the build-up of bank reserves rather than causing their growth, and that the downward pressure on reserves imposed by repayment of public sector debt to the banking sector can be nullified by bank operations affecting their holdings of reserves.

To illustrate the above discussion, and to indicate operations (in terms of *ex post* net changes in balance sheet figures) undertaken by the banks to limit or offset pressure on reserves generated by public sector borrowing from, or repayment of debt to, the banking sector, it is interesting to consider in some detail the relevant net adjustments that occurred in the month to mid-February 1978 and in the month to mid-June 1979.

In the month to mid-February 1978 repayment of public sector debt to the banking sector amounted to £882 million, whereas bank reserves decreased by £263 million. The banks' eligible liabilities increased by £546 million, causing the reserve ratio of the banking system to fall from 14·8 to 14·0 per cent, but since a fall in the reserve ratio is seasonally normal at that time of the year, it may be assumed that the recorded decrease in reserves was desired by, or at least acceptable to, the banks.

The banks' own holdings of public sector debt reserve assets (including balances with the Bank of England) decreased by £684 million, and money at call placed outside the discount market (fully secured by government debt) fell by £39 million. These decreases were partly balanced by (1) net acquisition of private sector reserve assets, viz. commercial bills (£7 million) and (2) an increase by £453 million of money at call placed with the discount market, of which £121 million represented a replacement of non-reserve loans repaid by the discount market (conversion of non-reserve into reserve assets) and £332 million represented new loans at call (creation of reserves within the banking sector). At the same time the discount market's holdings of public sector debt decreased by £450 million; this was largely repayment of debt by the government, though some of these assets may have been sold to the banks (the figure of £684 million previously mentioned showed net decrease in the banks' holdings of public sector debt reserve assets).Allowing for repayment of advances made by the Bank of England (£80 million), the running down of holdings of public sector debt provided the discount market with £370 million in addition to £332 million supplied by the banks. Discount houses, etc., used these funds to acquire private sector debt (including CDs – probably, largely, newly issued by the banks in conjunction with new call loans made by them – and placements in the interbank market) and to repay debts to non-bank suppliers of sterling funds. As a result of these operations of the discount houses, etc., new bank deposits were generated replacing those extinguished when used to make payments to the authorities and balancing new bank lending to the discount market.

In the month to mid-June 1979 public sector borrowing from the banking sector amounted to £115 million: the banks decreased holdings of public sector debt reserve assets (including balances with the Bank of England) by £5 million but increased holdings of public sector debt not having the status of reserve assets (including special deposits) by £84 million; the discount market acquired £121 million of assets issued by public sector debtors, and the Banking Department of the Bank of England reduced its holdings of public sector debt by £86 million (excluding changes being the counterpart of changes in bankers' deposits and special deposits). In the same month the banks' eligible liabilities rose by £574 million but their total reserves decreased by £23 million; the reserve ratio of the banking system fell from 13·5 to 13·3 per cent and was again at that level on the reporting date in July. This and the behaviour of reserve ratios of the principal groups of banks between May and July 1979 reporting dates suggest that the change recorded in June was approximately in accordance with the banks' wishes. In other words, it is reasonable to assume that the banks operated so as to cause a small decrease in their reserves – or, at least, that they considered such a decrease acceptable.

The banks reduced their holdings of British government stock with less than a year to final maturity by £56 million; it may be presumed that these stocks were disposed of to the authorities, the proceeds being credited to the banks' balances with the Bank of England. The banks used these funds and the amount (£75 million) by which they reduced their balances with the Bank of England as compared with the amount outstanding in mid-May (a total of £131 million) for three purposes: (1) to acquire notes from the Bank of England (£5 million); (2) to place special deposits (£21 million); and (3) to buy Treasury bills and local authority bills from the discount market, thus supplying the latter with funds to pay for newly issued Treasury bills (£105 million) (the banks may have bought some Treasury bills from the Bank of England's market agent). However, the banks acquired £126 million of Treasury and local authority bills, the purchase of £21 million being financed by reducing money at call to the discount market.[18] These operations together reduced bank reserves by £26 million, and changes in money at call placed outside the discount market (+£9 million) and in holdings of commercial bills (–£6 million) brought the total decrease in the banks' holdings of reserves to £23 million.

Discount houses, etc., disposed of a substantial amount of private sector debt and used the proceeds of these sales to acquire public sector debt and to repay some non-reserve bank loans as well as some loans made to them by non-bank suppliers of funds.

CHAPTER SIX

Control of the Stock of Money

Introduction

The stock of money consists of currency in circulation with the public and bank deposits – sterling current account deposits of the UK private sector (excluding banks) in the case of M1; sterling current account and time deposits and CDs of the UK private and public sectors in the case of sterling M3. Deposits constitute quantitatively the major part of the stock of money; moreover, the UK monetary authorities have long followed the practice of always meeting in full the public's demand for currency. Thus monetary control measures must be aimed at the volume of bank deposits, and the object of those measures must be to determine the magnitude of this monetary aggregate so that the sum of deposits and currency in circulation equals the desired stock of money. M3 is generally, though not universally, considered to be a more significant monetary aggregate than M1, and therefore measures of monetary policy aim at influencing the total of all types of bank deposits.

Elementary textbooks often give the impression that, if official action causes a change in the volume of bank reserves, then the banks gradually increase or decrease their deposits and assets in order to re-establish the equilibrium ratio of reserves to deposits. The approach, often called the bank credit multiplier approach, oversimplifies the problem. The fact is that the banks cannot increase or decrease deposits directly. If they wish to expand deposits the banks must induce the public to sell assets to them or to increase borrowing from them; if they find it necessary to contract deposits the banks must induce the public to buy assets from them (surrendering deposits in payment) and, unless they are prepared to operate a stringent loan rationing system, they must induce the public to reduce the volume of borrowing.

It is clear that the authors of the competition and credit control scheme considered that changes in the stock of money would come about in the course of a general process of portfolio adjustment caused by changes in interest rates. They saw the significance of the imposition (or relaxation) of pressure on the banks' reserve position in that it induced reactions by the banks which brought about, or strengthened, the necessary changes in interest rates. Thus, discussing the competition and credit control proposals in his address to the International Banking Conference in Munich in May 1971, the then Governor of the Bank of England said:

> It is not expected that the mechanism of the minimum asset ratio and Special Deposits can be used to achieve some precise multiple contraction or expansion of bank assets. Rather the intention is to use our control over liquidity, which these instruments will reinforce, to influence the structure of interest rates. The resulting changes in relative rates of return will then induce shifts in the asset portfolios of both the banks and the public.[1]

Shifts in the public's asset portfolios caused by a rise in interest rates must, broadly, consist of substitution of financial assets for money – the banks and, perhaps, the authorities themselves being the suppliers of financial assets. Since bank deposits surrendered by the public to the banks in payment for securities supplied are cancelled,[2] the contraction in the demand for money caused by a rise in interest rates is balanced by an equal decrease in the existing stock of money. *Mutatis mutandis*, shifts in the public's asset portfolios caused by a fall in interest rates must, in the aggregate, consist of substitution of money for other financial assets, the latter being absorbed by the banks and paid for by additions to the sellers' bank deposits. Thus, by inducing appropriate 'shifts in asset portfolios of the banks and the public', the authorities can increase or decrease the stock of money so as to bring it, approximately, to its desired level.

The Adjustment Process

The general nature of the process of monetary control sketched out in the preceding section is clear and straightforward. Indeed, it can be said that the volume of deposits cannot be reduced (increased) unless the banks can dispose of (acquire) assets, i.e. unless the public or the government are prepared to rearrange their portfolios accordingly. But the process itself must be examined in greater depth and some of its aspects must be highlighted to bring out their significance as essential parts of the transmission mechanism through which monetary pressure influences the flow of aggregate demand.

Official action to impose pressure on bank reserves normally takes the form of a call for special deposits rather than that of open market operations. There are two reasons for this.

(1) The authorities sell all the securities that can be sold to buyers outside the banking sector at the ruling level of interest rates in order to raise funds to finance public sector expenditure. Additional sales in order to reduce bank reserves are not feasible unless the authorities are willing to cause a temporary, sharp fall in gilt-edged prices – a policy to which they have long been opposed.
(2) Sales of Treasury bills to discount houses can always be increased and such operations are often used to cause short-term interest rates to rise. But their effects on bank reserves materialize slowly and gradually: they appear as discount houses reduce holdings of private sector debt and use the proceeds to repay Bank of England loans which they obtained to finance 'additional' purchases of Treasury bills.

As a result of placing special deposits the banks' holdings of eligible reserve assets decrease; it can be presumed that if the intention of the authorities is to cause monetary contraction the size of special deposits required is such as to decrease bank reserves so as to make reserve ratios *lower* than the banks desire to maintain (otherwise the measure would have little, if any, effect).

Individual banks respond to the disturbance in the structure of their assets by attempting to dispose of non-reserve assets which, because of their nature, can be quickly disposed of – i.e., they attempt to sell gilt-edged securities and other negotiable instruments from their portfolios and to withdraw funds placed at short term in the interbank market, in the market for temporary loans to local authorities and in the market for finance house deposits. They also try to issue new certificates of deposit and to attract new (wholesale) time deposits. Individual banks obtain payments in the form of claims on other banks, the settlement of which results in transfers of eligible reserve assets to the banks presenting these claims. All banks engage in these operations and therefore while some of them gain reserves others lose them but the volume of reserves in the banking system remains unchanged. But the reserve position of the banking system improves because the decrease in the banks' holdings of non-reserve assets is balanced by an equal fall in deposits.

The banking system as a whole disposes of gilt-edged securities and other marketable instruments by selling them to non-bank economic units which surrender deposits in payment. But the banking system as a whole can withdraw funds from parallel markets only if non-bank economic units supply funds (bank deposits) to debtors in these markets. The latter use deposits so acquired to repay the banks, and these deposits are then cancelled, balancing decreases in the banks' holdings of parallel market assets. It must be noted, however, that the banks press on debtors in parallel markets as soon as special deposits are called, i.e. before the flow of non-bank funds to their markets has developed. Those called upon to repay funds placed with them – banks, local authorities, finance houses – must make arrangements to discharge their obligations. They try to re-borrow by offering higher interest rates. Local authorities and finance houses are most likely to be successful because, if the banks insisted on repayment of market loans, these debtors would make use of standby overdraft facilities which they nearly always have. Banks unable to re-borrow in the interbank market must pay off their debts by surrendering reserve assets to creditor banks.

Operations outlined in the two preceding paragraphs are undertaken by the banks to ease reserve pressure by reducing deposits and holdings of non-reserve money market and gilt-edged assets. These effects are likely to be small, however, particularly at the early stages of the adjustment process. But the operations themselves are very significant and vitally important in the development of the adjustment process: their significance lies in the fact that they cause a rise in interest rates in the markets in which they take place.

There are two other tendencies which exert upward pressure on interest rates. (1) To place special deposits the banks must obtain cash. They get it by withdrawing money at call from the discount houses, forcing them to borrow from the Bank of England. Discount houses then make efforts to repay loans to the Bank of England: if they have borrowed on penal terms they naturally wish to eliminate these very expensive debts as soon as possible, but even if the Bank has assisted them at market rates they wish to reduce their indebtedness to it because being in debt to the Bank makes them very vulnerable to increases in interest rates which the authorities may wish to impose. Thus, discount houses try to reduce purchases of assets, to sell assets from their portfolios and to increase borrowing from market sources. These operations cause increases in interest rates in short-term markets. (2) Official operations in conjunction with special deposits – in particular, lending to discount houses and purchases of Treasury bills from banks and discount houses – are undertaken on terms consistent with the authorities' view on the desired level of interest rates; since in the context of restrictive action the authorities' aim is to raise interest rates, their operations must be expected to be conducted so as to intensify upward pressure on interest rates ruling in financial markets.

The rise, possibly a sharp rise, in gilt-edged yields and in interest rates quoted in the short-term financial markets affects yield differentials and increases the attractiveness of assets traded in these markets in relation to other assets. This tends to stimulate non-bank demand for assets that the banks and discount houses wish to discard,* and it follows that after interest rates have risen bank operations in non-reserve money market assets appear capable of causing a fall in deposits and non-reserve assets and thus of improving the reserve position of the banking system.

Non-bank financial intermediaries are the most important potential demanders of assets offered by the banks. They tend to be sensitive to changes in yield differentials, they have easy access to wholesale money markets, and they command large funds which they desire to invest or re-invest. Thus, a relative rise in short-term financial market rates is likely to induce non-bank financial intermediaries to increase the pro-

* It should be noted that effects of asset sales (to non-bank buyers) by the banks themselves and by discount houses may be significantly different: in the former case bank deposits decrease and this decrease is balanced by a reduction in bank holdings on *non-reserve* assets; in the latter case if discount houses use non-bank funds acquired to reduce their indebtedness to the Bank of England the resulting decrease in bank deposits is balanced by a fall in the banks' holdings of *reserve* assets – consequently the reserve position of the banks worsens. Moreover, assets supplied by the banks and by discount houses are, for the most part, close or fairly close substitutes, so that, given the total increase in non-bank demand for this category of assets, discount house asset sales represent largely diversion of available non-bank funds away from the banks. Thus, not only do successful asset disposals by discount houses weaken the reserve position of the banks, they also weaken the banks' ability to improve it.

portion of available funds (net current inflow of funds *plus* net maturities of assets) devoted to purchases of short-dated marketable instruments and to placements in parallel markets, at the same time correspondingly reducing other types of lending and purchases of other assets. This reaction is likely to be particularly strong if interest rates on those other loans and investments are expected to rise in the near future. Funds may also come from non-financial companies tempted by the rise in rates in parallel markets to place funds there instead of using them to expand trade credit or to increase stocks, etc.

If the operations to adjust bank assets and liabilities indicated in the preceding paragraph are successfully accomplished, their effects are very important. The fall in the volume of bank deposits constitutes a decrease in the stock of money. But more than that: to the extent that non-bank funds that flow to parallel markets (enabling debtors in these markets to repay the banks) and those that are used to buy gilt-edged securities and other assets directly from the banks have been withheld or withdrawn from private sector users, the fall in the volume of bank deposits represents a decrease in the aggregate amount of transactions balances held by the private sector. This decrease in transactions balances generates financial stringency, which prevents economic units directly affected from making outlays to expand their activities and may force some economic units to contract activities because they find themselves unable to maintain expenditure at the old level. Financial stringency tends to spread as economic units that would have been the recipients of payments that cannot now be made experience reductions in cash inflows and must, in turn, curtail their outlays. Thus, the flow of aggregate demand is damped down, which is, of course, the ultimate object of the policy of monetary restraint. Unfortunately, there are several reasons to believe that bank operations in financial markets are unlikely to induce substantial withdrawals of funds from use in the private sector and that, consequently, the effects of these operations in reducing volume of bank deposits and in damping down the flow of aggregate demand are likely to be weak. Even more unfortunately, these effects can turn perverse.

In the first place, short-maturity temporary loans to local authorities and deposits with finance houses are very close substitutes (in terms of liquidity, riskiness and capital value certainty) for various classes of interest-bearing time deposits with banks held as asset balances rather than transactions balances. This suggests that a part of the flow of non-bank funds to parallel markets induced by relative increases in interest rates in these markets is very likely to be substitution of parallel market assets for *idle* balances held as bank deposits. Deposits involved in this rearrangement of assets are, of course, surrendered to the banks and cancelled, but the resulting decrease in the volume of bank deposits represents a contraction in the *idle* component of the stock of money, which does not affect the flow of aggregate demand. Needless to say, the banks' reserve position improves whatever the original character of deposits surrendered to the banks.

Second, it is possible that the acquisition of assets disposed of by the banks (particularly their acquisition by non-bank financial intermediaries) may constitute a use of funds that would otherwise be devoted to purchases of public sector debt. The reason for this is that temporary loans to local authorities and finance house deposits are closer substitutes for new issues of short-term public sector debt than for loans to the private sector. This suggests that a rise in interest rates in parallel money markets, if not matched by a rise in yields on new issues of public sector debt, is more likely to cause a redirection of funds from the public sector via parallel markets to the banks than from the private sector to the banks. The fall in lending to the public sector, which this change in the use of funds by non-bank financial intermediaries and by other non-bank economic units implies, forces the government to increase, correspondingly, its borrowing from the banking sector and thus to increase the supply of new reserve assets to the banks. In short, the counterpart of the disposal of non-reserve assets by the banks is not a decrease in the volume of bank deposits but an increase in the banks' holdings of eligible reserve assets.* Thus, the pressure on the reserve position of the banking system eases and this reduces the magnitude of adjustment that the banks must accomplish.

Third, increases in interest rates caused by the banks' operations in

* If private sector deposits paid over to non-bank intermediaries are used by intermediaries to buy new issues of public sector debt, bank deposits decrease and bank reserves fall, but when the government spends the proceeds of sales of securities to intermediaries bank deposits are recreated and reserve assets flow back to the banks. If private sector deposits acquired by intermediaries are placed in parallel markets, thus enabling debtors in these markets to repay debts to the banks, bank deposits fall and this fall is balanced by an equal decrease in the banks' holdings of parallel market assets. Government spending is the same as in the preceding case, and thus deposits rise again and a flow of reserves to the banks takes place. But in this case this is a flow of new reserves, not a return of reserves to the banks. When all relevant transactions have taken place the volume of bank deposits is the same in both cases. But some deposits balanced by non-reserve assets in the former case are balanced by eligible reserve assets in the latter.

financial markets may attract internationally mobile funds. The entry of these funds into markets for sterling financial assets enables fund-takers in these markets to repay some of their debts to the banks. But either the exchange of foreign funds into sterling uses sterling deposits that otherwise would have flowed to the Exchange Equalization Account in net payments for foreign currencies (in which case, to the extent that foreign funds are invested in private sector debt, public sector borrowing from the overseas sector is reduced and its borrowing from the banking sector must be correspondingly increased), or the authorities must provide new sterling, which necessarily involves an increase in public sector borrowing from the banking sector. Thus, disposals by the banks of non-reserve assets are balanced not by a decrease in deposits but by an increase in holdings of eligible reserve assets. Indeed, if foreign funds are invested in CDs their inflow causes a rise in bank deposits and in reserves.[3]

It seems very probable that bank operations in non-reserve money market and gilt-edged assets improve the reserve position of the banking system, but that this improvement is only in a small measure due to a decrease in the volume of deposits and that, furthermore, a part of the fall in deposits reflects the transformation of idle balances from bank deposits into only slightly less liquid parallel market assets.

Finally, it must be noted that the banks sometimes try to improve their reserve position by attracting new deposits (and reserve assets) rather than by disposing of non-reserve assets from their portfolios (see chapter 2 above, pp. 25–6). While most of 'new' deposits are deposits attracted from other banks, some of them may be funds that would normally be used by their owners to buy new issues of public sector debt which have been attracted to the banks by high interest rates offered on CDs and large, fixed-term conventional bank deposits. The diversion of funds from the government to the banks increases public sector borrowing from the banking sector, thus causing a flow of additional reserve assets to the banks.

In so far as the adjustment process consists of bank operations in financial markets, its impact on the volume of deposits (decrease) is likely to be small or even very small. Nevertheless, this part of the adjustment process if very important, because by its very nature it exerts a strong upward pressure on market rates of interest. This is vital because the principal market interest rates govern the banks' base rates and, through base rates or directly, the rates of interest charged by the banks on overdrafts and other loans to customers. Thus, the rise in market rates is the foundation on which the second part of the adjustment process – the core of which is gradual reduction in the volume of bank advances – is based.

A rise (or, in the case of expansionary policy, a fall) in bank lending rates is a crucial feature of the adjustment process under the competition and credit control system. Since reductions in the banks' non-reserve market loans and investments cannot be expected to produce more than a minor decrease in the volume of bank deposits,[4] the bulk of the change in the stock of money must come about as a result of downward pressure on advances. But, it must be remembered, one of the reasons for the introduction of the competition and credit control system was to ensure that the allocation of financial resources is determined by the free operation of the market mechanism. This clearly implies that, whenever a damping down of the volume of bank (and finance house) credit is necessary, this must be achieved mainly by interest rate pressure. It follows that, in operational terms, bank lending rates must be pushed up to the level at which they bite, i.e. a level high enough to reduce the demand for credit, and that they must be maintained at a high level until the contraction in the volume of bank advances outstanding, or in the rate of growth of advances, in line with official wishes has been achieved. In the address already referred to the then Governor of the Bank of England made clear that this was the intention of the authorities by saying: 'no limitation is envisaged on the authorities' ability . . . to bring about sufficiently strong pressure on bank lending rates'.[5]

Changes in the total of bank advances and overdrafts outstanding occur as a result of new lending on the one hand and current repayment of loans on the other. With reference to a particular period, new lending can be defined as loan disbursements by the banks and the increase in the utilization of overdrafts by customers during the period in question. Similarly, repayment of loans consists of the surrender of bank deposits by borrowers to banks in discharge of loan liabilities, whether on the dates of maturity of term loans or whenever the amounts of overdrafts are reduced. In the context of restrictive monetary policy, the desired change in the total of bank advances is a contraction or, more probably in practice, a decrease in the rate of growth, which must be reflected respectively in an absolute decrease in the volume of bank deposits or in a fall in the rate at which the volume of bank deposits increases over time.

A downward change in advances outstanding occurs if new lending is reduced or if current repayment of loans increases. In a given short period of time new lending is the result of decisions to give loans and provide overdraft facilities taken some time previously; these decisions cannot normally be rescinded and therefore the banks cannot reduce the flow of new lending immediately. Nor can the banks immediately cause an increase in the flow of repayment of loans: they cannot unilaterally bring forward maturity dates of term loans, and although they have the formal right to cancel overdraft facilities at any time it is normally not practicable to exercise this right – in most cases the debtors do not have the ability to meet unexpected demands for repayment – and it would seldom be desirable to do so.[6]

Under competition and credit control arrangements the reduction of bank lending is seen as materializing as a result of damping down of the demand for advances caused by a rise in interest rates charged on bank loans and overdrafts. Quite clearly, if demand for bank credit is responsive to increases in interest rates in the range below the highest level to which the authorities are prepared to push bank lending rates, a sharp rise in interest rates charged by the banks on loans may damp down advances substantially and quickly. Both new lending and repayment of loans are likely to be affected – the former because the holders of overdraft facilities tend to reduce their use of these facilities as their increased cost makes activities financed in this manner less attractive, and the latter because the increased cost of overdrafts induces attempts to reduce their amounts as much as possible. In other words, the rise in the cost of finance deters some economic units from expanding their activities and induces some others to contract theirs. The outcome is a decrease in the flow of aggregate demand, which spreads more and more widely as the initial contraction of the flow of payments is reflected in reduced incomes causing further cuts in outlay, i.e. as a multiplier process develops. It must be stressed that the fall in the demand for bank credit is the *result* of decisions to reduce spending, not their cause.[7] A decrease in the demand for bank credit enables the banks to reduce net lending. If the pressure on interest rates is maintained for some time and, if necessary, intensified, current repayment of loans will eventually exceed new lending making net lending negative – and thus causing the amount of advances outstanding to decrease. This decrease must, of course, be balanced by an equal decrease in the volume of deposits, and so the stock of money is reduced. It must be emphasized that the efficiency and reliability of the adjustment mechanism just described depends crucially on the responsiveness of the demand for bank credit to changes in lending rates. The authors of the competition and credit control scheme took the view that this was normally fair over the range of practicable changes in lending rates. But hard evidence to support that view has never been produced. Moreover, under inflationary conditions demand for credit may be particularly unresponsive to changes in lending rates: this is so because, if inflationary expectations prevail, even very sharp increases in nominal interest rates may represent very mild increases in real interest rates, so that the change in the conditions of borrowing is inadequate to induce a significant decrease in the volume of desired borrowing.

The object of restrictive monetary policy is not normally to bring about an *absolute decrease* in the stock of money. The object is, rather, to reduce monetary growth, i.e. to lower the rate of growth of the stock of money, by causing a reduction in the rate at which the volume of bank deposits is being increased. The nature of the adjustment process is not affected by this reformulation of the object of policy; but net lending by the banks may remain positive in this case, and thus the accomplishment of the necessary banking adjustments is easier.

Restrictive Measures and the Rate of Monetary Growth

The effects of restrictive measures on the rate of growth of the volume of deposits (and therefore on the rate of growth of the stock of money) are more complex than they appear to be at first sight and must therefore be considered in some detail.

In the ordinary course of events, assuming that the banks' actual reserve ratios are their desired ratios, the growth of bank deposits is governed by the growth of the banking system's holdings of eligible reserve assets. Inflows of reserve assets to the banks generate surplus reserve holdings, and the banks, individually, take action to substitute higher yielding non-reserve assets for the surplus reserve assets; these operations go on until the resulting rise in deposits (and other eligible liabilities) causes such increases in the *desired* holdings of reserves that all surpluses of reserves are absorbed. If the (weighted) average reserve ratio of the banking system remains unchanged, and if, in the aggregate, reserve leakages bear a stable relation to the growth of deposits, then the rate of growth of the volume of deposits must be equal to the rate at which the banks as a group increase their holdings of reserve assets.*

The placing of special deposits reduces the banks' actual reserve ratios making them lower than desired. Thus, even if the rate of net inflow (per cent per reporting period) of reserve assets to the banks is not reduced by restrictive policy measures, the banks' ability to create new deposits (eligible liabilities) is reduced. This is so for two reasons. (1) In the absence of special deposits the whole net inflow of reserve assets to the banks is available to satisfy reserve requirements (at the ratio or ratios desired by the banks) in respect of new deposits – those that are the counterpart of the net inflow of reserves and those generated by current bank operations made possible by the net inflow of reserves. If the banks are required to place special deposits, however, a part of the net inflow of reserves must be surrendered, period after period, to the Bank of England to make special deposits in respect of current increases in eligible liabilities.[8] Thus, increases in the banks' holdings of reserve assets (net acquisitions of reserves) are smaller than net inflows; this, clearly, restricts the banks' ability to expand assets and eligible liabilities. (2) The actual reserve ratio is lower than the desired ratio and the banks must be presumed to wish to raise the former to the level of the latter. To achieve this the banks must, as soon as conditions permit, retain as reserves some of the net acquisition of reserves, in addition to the normal retention needed to support current increases in eligible liabilities at the desired reserve ratio.

The continuing pressures exerted by special deposits on the reserve position of the banks force them to reduce the rate of lending so as to slow down expansion in the volume of deposits. It is the slowing down of expansion in the volume of deposits that eventually enables the banks to restore equilibrium ratios between holdings of reserve assets and the total of eligible liabilities outstanding and between increases in reserves and in eligible liabilities. The establishment of the new equilibrium is, of course, gradual, and the situation immediately after the placement of

* In subsequent discussion, for simplicity, movements of reserves will be expressed as net inflows, i.e. inflows *less* maturities, disposals and outflows owing to leakages. A net inflow *less* surrender of reserve assets to make special deposits will be called net acquisition of reserve assets.

special deposits must be distinguished from that which obtains some time later.

It was pointed out in the preceding section that the banks cannot immediately reduce net lending (overdrafts and advances); this being so, for some time, a large part of the total acquisition of non-reserve assets by the banks and the consequent creation of new deposits must be expected to continue at the old rate. Thus, at this stage of the process, the rate of growth of the total volume of bank deposits can fall only as a result of surrender of deposits to the banks, which is the counterpart of the disposal by the banks of gilt-edged securities and parallel market assets. This effect is unlikely to be strong, and consequently the banks' actual reserve ratios, which were sharply reduced by the placing of special deposits, improve very little (if at all) at this stage of the process unless bank operations in parallel markets cause an increase in the flow of reserve assets to the banks – see pp. 79–81 above. Thus, the placement of special deposits with the Bank of England and adjustments immediately following that placement may cause a slight fall in the rate of growth of bank deposits or it may leave that rate unchanged. And the reserve position of the banking system is likely to be unsatisfactory.

After some time, when the lag in the reaction of the demand for advances to the rise in lending rates has elapsed, net lending by means of overdrafts and other loans to customers decreases. This, together with decreases in the rates at which the banking system acquires other non-reserve assets, causes a fall in the rate of growth of bank deposits. The (eventual) restoration of equilibrium requires that this rate decreases sufficiently to make current net inflow of reserve assets to the banks adequate to support current expansion in the volume of deposits *and* to provide for special deposits in respect of the growth of eligible liabilities. During the process of adjustment (after the expiry of the lag in the reaction of the demand for advances) the rate of growth of eligible liabilities must be lower than the equilibrium rate determined by the rate of net inflow of reserve assets. This is necessary so that the banks can gradually raise actual reserve ratios until desired levels of these ratios are reached. The timing of this build-up of reserves in relation to eligible liabilities (when it can begin in relation to the time at which special deposits were introduced and how long it lasts) depends on the sharpness of the fall in the rate of growth of deposits on the one hand and on the kind and magnitude of changes (if any) in the rate of net inflow of reserves on the other.

The former is governed primarily by the magnitude and speed of response of the demand for bank credit to increases in lending rates: the rate of growth of deposits is most likely to fall more the stronger and the more rapid is the response of demand for bank credit. The banks can influence it a little by raising lending rates more if they expect the response of the demand for credit to be weak, or less if they expect it to be strong.

The latter is governed by a number of factors, the most important among them being the magnitude of government borrowing from (or repayment of debt to) the banking sector, and the ability and willingness of the banks and discount houses to engage in reserve-creating operations. If the government borrowing from the banking sector is substantial it is likely to be easy for the banks to increase the rate of net inflow of reserves by increasing the proportion of government debt eligible as reserve assets (directly or at one remove) in the total of public sector debt they take as lenders. On the other hand, if the government repays debt to the banks the latter's holdings of reserve assets tend to shrink and the banks may not be able to offset this shrinkage by market purchases of such assets and reserve-creating operations. The rate of net inflow of reserves to the banks is likely to decrease in such a case and may become negative. But it must be noted that government borrowing from the banking sector generates new deposits and partly offsets the downward tendency in deposit creation owing to lower net lending; repayment of government debt to the banks sharpens the fall in the rate of growth of the volume of deposits.

It follows from the foregoing that transition to the new equilibrium position may proceed according to any one of a large number of possible adjustment patterns; the specific pattern in a particular case depends on all the relevant circumstances, which are likely to differ from case to case. But the essential features of adjustment are the same in all cases and a very simple model can be used to highlight them.

Suppose that the net inflow of eligible reserve assets to the banks takes place at a constant rate (per cent per reporting period), and that this rate is the same before the call for special deposits is made by the authorities and after. In the absence of special deposits, the function $E_t = E_0 (1+u)^t$ (plotted in logarithmic form in figure 3) shows the time path of the banks' holdings of eligible reserve assets; E_0 represents holdings at the base time t_0, u is the rate of growth of reserves, and time is measured in reporting periods. When special deposits are operative the function no longer shows actual holdings of reserves but continues to indicate net inflows of reserve assets. In the absence of special deposits, and if the banks maintain a constant reserve ratio (desired = actual), the volume of eligible liabilities (assumed to consist of deposits only) is a constant multiple of holdings of reserves, viz. $D_t = \frac{E_t}{R}$ (where R is the desired reserve ratio). Thus $D_t = \frac{E_0(1+u)^t}{R}$ is the original equilibrium time path of the volume of deposits, and it is assumed that, until the time when special deposits are required to be made, it is also the actual time path of deposits. The rate of growth of the volume of deposits is u, the same as the rate of growth of reserves.

The use of the instrument of special deposits alters the equilibrium time path of the volume of bank deposits.

If special deposits are lodged without lag, i.e. at each reporting date in respect of deposits (eligible liabilities) outstanding at that reporting date, then the equilibrium volume of deposits at the end of each reporting period (D'_t) can be determined directly by using an adaptation of the bank credit multiplier formula. Thus:

$$D'_t = \frac{E_t - sD'_t}{R}$$

$$= \frac{E_0(1+u)^t}{R} - \frac{sD'_t}{R}$$

where sD'_t is the amount of special deposits with respect to the equilibrium volume of deposits; $E_0\ (1+u)^t - sD'_t$ is the amount of reserves needed to maintain D'_t given the rate of special deposits s and the desired reserve ratio R.

Rearranging,

$$D'_t\left(1+\frac{s}{R}\right) = \frac{E_0(1+u)^t}{R}$$

$$D'_t = \frac{E_0(1+u)^t}{R+s}$$

Assuming that reserves and deposits increase steadily between reporting dates, E_0, D_t and D'_t can be presented as continuous curves (or, in logarithmic form, as continuous straight lines) – their time paths.

In fact, special deposits are placed with a lag of one reporting period, i.e. the amount that must be lodged at reporting date t is calculated with respect to eligible liabilities outstanding at reporting date $t-1$. The equilibrium volume of deposits can be determined in this case by formulating and solving a difference equation. Thus:

$$D''_t = \frac{E_t - sD''_{t-1}}{R}.$$

That is to say,

$$D''_t = -\frac{s}{R}D''_{t-1} + \frac{E_0(1+u)^t}{R}$$

The initial condition is the equilibrium volume of deposits at the reporting date t^* (when special deposits are first lodged) – the amount of special deposits placed at that time is calculated by reference to the actual volume of deposits outstanding at t^*-1 (equilibrium volume before the use of the special deposits instrument). It should be noted that, since the D''_t function exists only from time t^*, it is convenient to use the notation $(t_n - t^*)$ for the numbering of reporting periods relevant to that function only, retaining notation t where the reference is to the overall time scale. t^* is of course a specific t; e.g., $t^* = 3$. Thus D''_0 is written $D''_{t^*-t^*}$:

$$D''_{t^*-t^*} = \frac{E_{t^*} - sD_{t^*-1}}{R} \qquad (D_{t^*-1} \text{ is known at time } t^*)$$

Using this initial condition, the solution of the difference equation for D''^*_t is:

$$D''^*_{t-t^*} = \left[D''_{t^*-t^*} - \frac{E_0(1+u)^{t^*}}{R+s}\right]\left(-\frac{s}{R}\right)^{(t-t^*)} + \frac{E_0(1+u)^t}{R+s}$$

The quotient s/R can be taken to be smaller than unity,[9] and it appears in the equation with a negative sign. Thus the equilibrium volume of deposits fluctuates about its long-run equilibrium level, the fluctuations are damped and eventually disappear. The long-run equilibrium of $D''^*_{t-t^*}$ is the equilibrium time path D'_t, the path relevant if special deposits are made without lag.

Figure 3 illustrates the foregoing discussion. The equations and the graph clearly show that, by using the instrument of special deposits, the

FIGURE 3

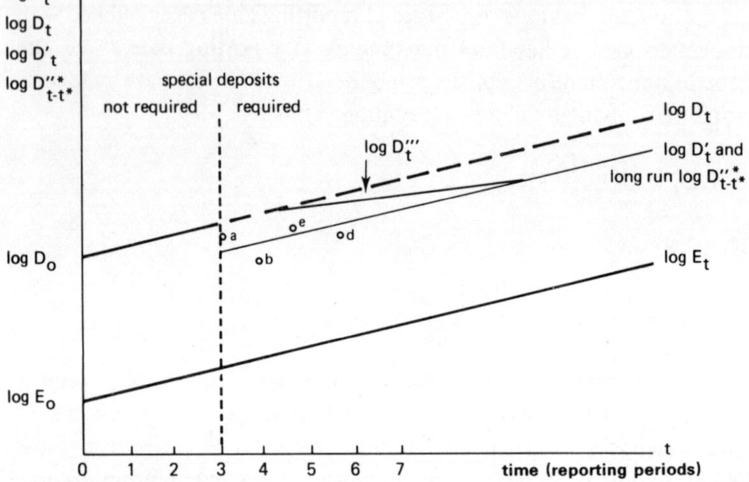

$\log E_t = \log E_0 + t.\log(1+u)$.

$\log D_t = \log E_0 + t.\log(1+u) - \log R$ (relevant if special deposits are not required).

$\log D'_t = \log E_0 + t.\log(1+u) - \log(R+s)$. In the long-run equilibrium, $\log D''^{*}_{t-t^*} = \log D'_t$

Points *a*, *b*, *c*, *d*, etc., indicate $\log D''^{*}_{t-t^*}$ before its equilibrium value is closely approached.

$\log D'''_t$ shows the time path of the actual level of deposits; it is not specified – see p. 87.

authorities can lower the equilibrium time path of the volume of bank deposits. But, apart from damped fluctuations in the short run caused by the lag with which special deposits are placed, the rate of growth (per cent per reporting period) of the equilibrium volume of bank deposits is unaffected – it is governed by the rate of net inflow of reserve assets to the banks.

The actual time path of the volume of bank deposits after the introduction of special deposits is, of course, very different from the equilibrium time path. It is very probable that initially it will not be changed at all, continuing along path D_t (broken line). But after a short lag decreases in net bank lending owing to higher interest rates and the slowing down of bank purchases of non-reserve assets owing to the tightness of the banks' reserve position will make the actual time path of deposits deviate from path D_t downward; i.e., there will be a fall in the actual rate of growth of deposits, a fall that is likely to increase in magnitude as the effects of restrictive policy measures spread.

It must be noted that, as long as the actual time path of deposits is above their equilibrium time path, the reserve position of the banks remains unsatisfactory. Special deposits are made in respect of actual increases in eligible liabilities and therefore are greater than they would have been if eligible liabilities (deposits) had grown according to their equilibrium path. Thus, in absolute terms, the deficiency of reserves (desired holdings of reserve assets given eligible liabilities outstanding *less* actual holdings) grows because net acquisitions of reserve assets (net inflows *less* placements of special deposits) are inadequate to maintain desired reserve ratios in respect of new deposits and other eligible liabilities. Nevertheless, the overall reserve ratios are likely to improve somewhat.

The fall in the actual rate of growth of the volume of deposits, indicated graphically by the flattening of line log D_t''' in figure 3,* eventually makes the actual volume of deposits smaller than equilibrium volume at the same date (the actual time path of the volume of deposits crosses the equilibrium path from above). Then, and only then, the banks are able to eliminate, gradually, their reserve deficiency by using a fraction of net acquisitions of reserve assets for that purpose. As reserve deficiency is reduced and approaches elimination, the banks can increase net lending – by reducing lending rates and by easing other conditions and requirements – and the result is an increase in the actual rate of growth of the volume of deposits. For a time this rate is likely to be somewhat higher than the equilibrium rate and thus the actual volume of deposits approaches the equilibrium volume of deposits (the two time paths merge); thereafter the volume of deposits grows at the equilibrium rate which, as has already been said, is governed by the rate of net inflow of eligible reserve assets to the banks.

In short: by using the instrument of special deposits the authorities can 'permanently' lower the equilibrium time path of the volume of bank deposits and therefore that of the stock of money; but if the rate of net inflow of reserves to the banks is unchanged they cannot, by means of special deposits, reduce the equilibrium rate of growth of the volume

* D'''_t function has not been specified because such specification can be made only on the basis of assumptions (or information) about a number of relationships, e.g. interest elasticity of the demand for bank loans, the structure of government borrowing, bank operations in parallel markets, etc.

of bank deposits. On the other hand, adjustments caused by special deposits tend to bring about a fall in the actual rate of growth of bank deposits. Although this fall is only temporary, the lower growth rate may persist long enough to restrain the growth of aggregate demand for a period of sufficient length to be significant. It is, of course, the fall in the actual rate of growth of bank deposits that makes possible the transition from the original equilibrium time path of total deposits to the new and lower equilbrium time path.

It must be noted that the effects summarized in the preceding paragraph depend to a large extent on the assumption that the rate of net inflow of reserves to the banks remains unchanged. An increase in the rate of net inflow of reserves, whether owing to deliberate action of the banks or to other causes, is virtually certain to weaken these effects and may completely nullify them. This is so because the easing of the banks' reserve positions is most likely to cause a decrease in interest rates including bank lending rates, thus partly or wholly lifting the pressure on the demand for credit and on bank lending and resulting in a recovery in the rate at which new deposits are created.

CHAPTER SEVEN

Special Deposits, 1972–78

Under competition and credit control arrangements monetary control is exercised by manipulating the level and structure of interest rates. Given stable reserve ratios of the banks, the role of special deposits is to reinforce official influence over interest rates. Special deposits fulfil their role by affecting the reserve position of the banks and thus forcing or inducing them to change the pattern of their operations.

The rate of interest policy is a continuous policy, the object of which is to cause a movement of interest rates towards, or to prevent them from moving away from, the levels considered by the authorities to be most appropriate given internal and external conditions and pressures.

From time to time the authorities find it necessary to change their policy stance: to take action to prevent or correct undesirable trends, such as excessive monetary expansion or undue sluggishness of monetary growth. It is in such circumstances that official influence over interest rates requires reinforcement by the use of special deposits; this is so because the object of policy is to combat market tendencies. In the present chapter the effects of special deposits (other than supplementary special deposits, which will be considered later) as an instrument for influencing interest rates by affecting the reserve position of the banking system will be discussed and appraised. Four occasions when the authorities attempted to impose restraint on the system will be considered (in November and December 1972, July 1973, November 1973 and September and October 1976), and two occasions when they eased their policy stance (in January and April 1974, and in January 1977).

The technique of temporary releases and recalls of special deposits for smoothing purposes will also be briefly commented on.

The Effects of Special Deposits[1]

General analysis of the working of the monetary system suggests that recourse by the authorities to the instrument of special deposits can be expected to be followed by: (1) a rise in short-term market rates of interest and an upward adjustment of the banks' base rates; (2) a decrease in the rate of bank lending to the private sector, owing partly to the impact of the rise in lending rates on the demand for bank credit and partly to the pressure on the banks' reserve position; (3) a decrease in the rate of monetary growth, reflecting the fall in the rate of creation of bank deposits consequent upon the lowering of the rate of bank lending.

On 9 November 1972 the Bank of England called for special deposits of 1 per cent of the banks' eligible liabilities to be lodged in two equal instalments on 30 November and 14 December. Then on 31 December 1972 the Bank of England made a second call for special deposits, amounting to 2 per cent of eligible liabilities, to be placed with the Bank in equal instalments on 3 and 17 January 1973.

The effect on interest rates was slow to appear; in spite of mild official pressure (official loans for smoothing purposes were given for seven days instead of overnight), interest rates did not rise significantly until the end of November when, following the placement of the first instalment of special deposits, rates in the discount market rose by close to $\frac{1}{4}$ per cent and those in parallel markets by rather more than $\frac{1}{4}$ per cent. The rise in short-term market rates continued throughout December and January: this tendency was engendered partly by special deposits which the banks had to place during that period and partly by official tactics in the market (assistance being given on rather stiff terms and increases in the amounts of Treasury bills offered). London clearing banks raised their base rates from 7 per cent at the end of November to $7\frac{1}{4}$ per cent in the middle of December, to $8\frac{1}{2}$ per cent in January 1973 and to $9\frac{1}{2}$ per cent in the middle of February.

The banks' reserve position did not actually deteriorate between reporting dates in November 1972 and in January 1973 – in fact, the combined reserve ratio of the banks was higher in December and

January than it had been in November. But it is clear that, if special deposits of £683 million had not been taken from banks, their reserves would have risen sharply,* and this might well have induced the banks to expand credit on a considerable scale. Special deposits greatly reduced the banks' ability to do so.

The interpretation of changes in the rate of growth of sterling advances to UK customers is greatly complicated by the fact that in January and February 1973 interest rates on CDs and some types of wholesale term deposits exceeded blue chip lending rates, thus making possible arbitrage operations in overdrafts and CDs. Such operations (often called the overdraft–CD merry-go-round or round tripping) did take place at that time, and because of them recorded increases in the rate of growth of advances in January and February overstate the magnitude of the expansion of bank lending.[2] Similarly, very sharp recorded decreases in the rate of growth of advances in the months to mid-March and mid-April (when that rate turned negative) are partly spurious, reflecting the unwinding of arbitrage positions. Nevertheless, it appears probable that the rate of growth of advances genuinely decreased as compared with January and February and was perhaps rather lower than it had been between mid-September and mid-December 1972. It is legitimate to conclude that official policy, of which special deposits were an important element, had a significant restraining effect on the rate of growth of bank lending to the private sector.

Rates of growth of broad monetary aggregates fluctuate considerably from month to month; quarterly figures tend to be more significant. A comparison of the period of three months ending in mid-January (before the introduction of the policy of restraint) and the period of three months to mid-April (when the policy of restraint was operative) shows that the rate of growth of the stock of money (M3) decreased from 6·67 to 4·68 per cent per three months. Rates of growth of other important monetary aggregates, e.g. total sterling deposits (excluding interbank deposits but including all CDs issued) and sterling deposits of UK residents other than banks *plus* CDs held outside the banking system, showed changes of the same kind and similar magnitude.

Changes in the growth rates of monetary aggregates represent the

* In December 1972 some £500 million gilt-edged securities held by the banks passed the 'one year to maturity' line and became eligible reserve assets; there was also substantial government borrowing from the banks at the turn of the year.

combined result of all relevant influences. In the case now under discussion it must be observed that, in the three months to mid-April 1973, bank lending to both the public and the private sector was smaller than in the three months to mid-January 1973. But the former decreased by £399 million (from £278 million to −£121 million), and the latter by £154 million (from £1,333 million to £1,179 million). Clearly, the fall in public sector borrowing from the banks was a more important influence in damping down the rate of monetary expansion than was the decrease in bank lending to the private sector. But, equally clearly, it is only the latter that could be influenced by monetary policy of restraint. On the other hand, in the autumn of 1972 there were indications of impending expansion of bank lending to the private sector, and it is probable that such expansion would have taken place if the authorities had not acted to raise interest rates and withdraw reserves from the banking system.

It is legitimate to conclude that the use of the special deposits instrument in November and December 1972 caused a rise in interest rates and damped down somewhat the expansion of bank lending to the private sector and that in the latter respect recorded figures may fail to indicate the true magnitude of the restraint exerted.

On 19 July 1973 the Bank of England called for special deposits amounting to 1 per cent of the banks' eligible liabilities to be lodged in two equal instalments on 6 and 15 August. At the same time the authorities increased sharply the offers of Treasury bills for tender,[3] thus causing a fall in tender prices (a rise in rates demanded).[4] Moreover, the authorities let it be known that they desired to see a sharp rise in the minimum lending rate.[5]

In the second half of July interest rates in the discount market rose by about 4 per cent, but in the parallel markets principal rates rose by under 3 per cent. In the three weeks ending on 24 August, however, discount market rates rose only a little, but parallel market rates went up again by close to 3 per cent. It is reasonable to infer from this pattern of movements of market interest rates that in the second half of July increases were caused mainly by the manipulation of the issue of Treasury bills and other official operations in the discount market, but that in August increases in interest rates were influenced by bank operations made necessary by the placements of special deposits. Upward movement of market interest rates caused London clearing banks to raise base rates from 8 to 10 per cent at the very beginning of August, and then to 11 per cent in the third week of that month.

At first sight it appears that the placements of special deposits on 6 and 15 August weakened the banks' reserve position. From mid-April to mid-July the combined reserve ratio of the banking system was maintained at not less than 14 per cent and the ratio of London clearing banks stood a little above the combined ratio. At the mid-August reporting date, however, the combined ratio was 13·4 per cent, and that of London clearing banks 13 per cent (it had been 14·2 per cent a month earlier); and it was not until mid-November that these ratios returned to their pre-August levels. But it must be observed that the rate of growth of eligible liabilities of the banking system was virtually the same in the three months after the call for special deposits as it had been in the three months before the call (7·31 and 7·47 per cent respectively), and that eligible liabilities of the London clearing banks grew more in the three months after the call (9·99 per cent) than in the three months before it (7·26 per cent). The banks' behaviour indicates that they did not consider that they were under serious reserve pressure. It should also be noted that, whereas in the three months ending in mid-July the banks increased their holdings of reserve assets by 5·08 per cent, in the three months from mid-July reserve holdings rose by 5·31 per cent in spite of the outflow of reserve assets owing to placements of special deposits. It is likely that the ability of the banks to acquire additional reserve assets enabled them to maintain unchanged the rate of growth of eligible liabilities.

The monetary measures of restraint taken in July 1973 had the direct effects expected of them – interest rates rose and the banks' reserve position temporarily tightened slightly – but they do not seem to have damped down expansion of bank lending to the private sector. The rate of growth of sterling advances to UK residents was very high in the month to mid-July. It fell sharply in the month to mid-August, but that, clearly, was too soon after policy action was taken to have been caused by that action. It fell again in the month to mid-September: perhaps this result was influenced in some measure by high lending rates and the general tightness of the financial situation. But in the month to mid-October the rate of growth of advances rose again, although London clearing banks' base rates remained unchanged (at 11 per cent). It appears that in the late summer and autumn of 1973 special deposits and other monetary measures failed to restrain monetary expansion, which was fed much more by lending to the private sector than to the public sector.

The authorities were dissatisfied with the effects produced by measures taken in July, and on 13 November 1973 the Bank of England made a call for special deposits amounting to 2 per cent of eligible liabilities to be lodged with the Bank in four equal instalments on 30 November, 12 December, 27 December 1973 and 2 January 1974. At the same time the minimum lending rate was raised from $11\frac{1}{4}$ to 13 per cent by an *administrative* decision of the authorities (the usual formula was temporarily suspended).

Interest rates responded immediately and sharply in both the discount market and the parallel markets. Moreover, London clearing banks at once raised their base rates by 2 per cent to 13. Market rates then continued to rise, especially those in parallel markets because the banks expected and, later, experienced a tightening of the reserve position and competed keenly for deposits and reserve assets. Between 9 November and 14 December the main parallel market rates rose by close to 4 per cent. Increases in interest rates were due partly to the sharp raising of the minimum lending rate, other official operations and moral suasion but the pressure on banks caused by special deposits also played an important part.

The banks' reserve position deteriorated between the reporting date in November and that in December: the combined reserve ratio of the banking system fell from 14·3 to 13·8 per cent and that of London clearing banks from 14·5 to 13·8 per cent. In view of the fact that the banks, particularly the clearing banks, tend to build up their holdings of reserve assets at the end of the year – in anticipation of reserve outflows through cutomers' tax payments in January, February and March – it is clear that by taking special deposits the authorities made the banks' reserve position uncomfortably tight. If the third and fourth instalments of special deposits had not been cancelled, the pressure on bank reserves would have been severe.

The effects of the November 1973 measures on bank lending to the private sector and on the behaviour of monetary aggregates cannot be meaningfully assessed. On 17 December 1973 the Bank of England announced the introduction of a new instrument of monetary control – supplementary special deposits (discussed in the next chapter);

operations became strongly affected by the new rules and by the pressures generated by these rules. The new arrangements deprived ordinary special deposits of much of their significance, and for this reason the Bank of England revoked the original call in respect of special deposits due to be lodged on 27 December 1973 and 2 January 1974.

A more specific difficulty of interpretation of information relating to the first quarter of 1974 is, of course, the highly abnormal character of the economic position at that time: the rise in oil prices, the miners' strike, the three-day week and, later, political uncertainty severely distorted economic relationships and disrupted monetary and financial flows. Moreover, partly because of the abnormality of the economic situation, the authorities eased their policy stance – several releases of special deposits were made between January and April 1974. But the clearing banks' base rates remained unchanged.

In the summer of 1976 the supplementary special deposits scheme was not operative and the authorities decided to enforce monetary restraint by traditional means. On 10 September 1976 the minimum lending rate was pushed up from 11½ to 13 per cent, and on 16 September the Bank of England called for special deposits amounting to 1 per cent of the banks' eligible liabilities to be lodged with the Bank in two equal instalments on 29 September and 6 October. On 7 October the minimum lending rate was raised by administrative action from 13 to 15 per cent, and at the same time a call was made for special deposits to be lodged in two equal instalments on 2 and 15 November. The second instalment was twice postponed and finally cancelled when other influences caused a severe tightening of the reserve position of the banks and stringent conditions in the money market in December 1976 and January 1977.

The first rise in the minimum lending rate caused an immediate upward adjustment of interest rates in the discount and parallel markets, and the upward movement continued until the beginning of October. Increases in parallel market rates were only a little greater than in rates on assets traded in the discount market and this rather suggests that these increases were due mainly to the pervasive influence of the minimum lending rate strengthened by official market tactics; special deposits and bank operations connected with them were probably of secondary importance in this connection. London clearing banks increased their base rates from 10½ to 12 per cent.

The second (administrative) rise in the minimum lending rate caused the upward movement of market rates to continue, and this induced London clearing banks to raise their base rates to $13\frac{1}{2}$ per cent and then to 14 per cent. Interest rates both in the discount market and in parallel markets reached their peaks in the last week of October and eased a little at the beginning of November when the banks lodged special deposits. It appears that in the autumn of 1976 special deposits had comparatively little effect on interest rates.

The impact of the October and November 1976 placements of special deposits on the reserve position of the banking system was negligible. The recorded falls in the combined reserve ratio and in the total of reserve assets held by the banking system give a misleading impression. They were due to the fact that accepting houses and 'other' British banks reduced their holdings of reserve assets by amounts far in excess of their placements of special deposits. It appears that, by doing so, these two groups of banks supplied reserve assets to other groups (in particular to London clearing banks) and thus enabled them to place special deposits and to increase holdings of reserves at the same time. The reserve ratio of London clearing banks at 13·6 and 13·5 per cent in October and November was higher than it had been in September and not significantly lower than in October and November 1975. The ratio of Scottish clearing banks showed only a slight decline.

Bank lending in sterling to the private sector (seasonally adjusted) rose substantially in the month to mid-September and again in the month to mid-October. But in the three months that followed it decreased steadily, being in each month smaller than it had been in the preceding month. It appears probable that this trend was caused by the damping down of the demand for credit by increases in and/or high levels of bank lending rates. If this was so then, clearly, the rate of interest policy pursued by the authorities in September and October was successful in restraining expansion of bank credit. But it must be noted that special deposits do not appear to have greatly reinforced the policy to raise interest rates and cannot therefore be given much credit for contributing to the imposition of restraint on bank lending to the private sector.

The seasonally adjusted rate of growth of sterling M3 decreased steadily from mid-September 1976 to mid-February 1977, being negative in the last three months of that period. A progressive decrease in bank lending to the private sector contributed to this trend, but the main cause of it, and particularly of the negative rate of monetary growth at the end of the period, was the substantial repayment of public sector (mainly central government) debt to the banking sector. Rates of growth of total sterling deposits (excluding interbank deposits) and of sterling deposits of UK non-bank holders *plus* CDs held outside the banking sector moved in broadly the same way as the growth rate of sterling M3.

As an instrument of monetary restraint, special deposits do not appear to be either strong or reliable. Their placement by the banks tends to generate pressure on financial markets and to cause interest rates to rise. Thus, they are a useful adjunct to the policy of manipulating interest rates. But their impact on the reserve position of the banks tends to be very weak. Usually the banks' holdings of reserve assets decrease a little immediately after placements of special deposits are made and reserve ratios fall. But the banks appear able to increase the rate at which they add to their holdings of reserve assets, and consequently they can rebuild their reserves very quickly. The rebuilding of reserves obviates the need for enforcing significant reductions (even temporary ones) in the rate of growth of eligible liabilities. Moreover, while reserve ratios of the London and Scottish clearing banks are fairly stable, the banks are willing to allow significant month-to-month variations. The banks' willingness to allow moderate temporary decreases in their reserve ratios obviates the need for immediate action to reduce eligible liabilities when holdings of reserves have fallen. It follows, of course, that special deposits can only cause a decrease in the stock of money, or in the rate of growth, indirectly, by making interest rates rise sufficiently to damp down the demand for bank loans.

Releases of Special Deposits

In January 1974 the authorities, having provided themselves with a new instrument of monetary pressure – supplementary special deposits – found themselves able to use (ordinary) special deposits more freely and more flexibly. On 31 January 1974 the Bank of England announced that special deposits amounting to $\frac{1}{2}$ per cent of eligible liabilities would be released on 4 February. The authorities wished to replenish the banks' holdings of reserves which were being depleted by unexpectedly large tax payments. They wished to prevent the reserve position becoming very tight, as this would cause a further rise in interest rates which was judged undesirable from the domestic point of view and was not necessary for external reasons (foreign interest rates eased a little at that time).

Interest rates drifted down slowly in both the discount market and the parallel markets, but to begin with decreases in rates were small. They were greater in the second half of February, and this was, perhaps, due partly to the fact that the banks' reserve position (as reported on 20 February) was comparatively easy; but official purchases of Treasury, local authority and commercial bills in the market and placements of funds by the Bank of England in the market for temporary loans to local authorities probably constituted a more important influence on market rates.

Monetary trends were unexpectedly satisfactory in the first three months of 1974. The seasonally adjusted quarterly rate of growth of M3 was 3 per cent in the first quarter of 1974 (the bulk of this increase took place in January) compared with 8·1 and 7·2 per cent in the third and fourth quarters of 1973 respectively. Bank lending to the private sector (whether unadjusted or seasonally adjusted) was substantially smaller in the first quarter of 1974 than it had been in each of the last two quarters of 1973.[6] The introduction of the supplementary special deposits scheme had a strong impact: the growth of the banks' interest-bearing eligible liabilities, which had been vigorous in the last three months of 1973, was brought to a halt: IBELs were no higher in March 1974 than they had been in January and were lower than in February. In these circumstances the authorities decided to release special deposits on 8 April, 16 April and 22 April – $\frac{1}{2}$ per cent of eligible liabilities on each occasion.

The announcement of releases produced an immediate sharp drop in interest rates,[7] particularly in parallel money markets where principal interest rates decreased by $1\frac{1}{2}$–$1\frac{3}{4}$ per cent. The first release of special deposits (on 8 April) was followed by further falls in market rates of the order of $\frac{1}{2}$ per cent, but the two releases that took place later in April do not seem to have affected market rates. Decreases in market rates induced London clearing banks to reduce their base rates by $\frac{1}{2}$ per cent. Market interest rates continued to drift down throughout May, and the base rates of London clearing banks were reduced again by $\frac{1}{2}$ per cent.

In the months to mid-April and to mid-May there was a substantial repayment of sterling debt by the central government to the banks.

Releases of special deposits cushioned the impact of this repayment on bank reserves, which might otherwise have come under severe strain. In the month to mid-June it was the rest of the public sector that repaid debt to the banks, and this was reflected partly in decreases in the banks' holdings of non-reserve assets.

In the three months to mid-June bank lending to the private sector (unadjusted) was somewhat smaller than in the preceding three months and only a little higher on the comparison of seasonally adjusted figures.

Net repayment of public sector debt to the banks and the moderate scale of bank lending to the private sector combined to produce very low rates of monetary growth. In the months to mid-April, mid-May and mid-June seasonally adjusted M3 rose by 0·1, 0·3 and –0·3 per cent; in the second quarter of 1974 it rose by 1·8 per cent.

At the end of 1976 bank lending to the private sector had been severely restrained by the policy of high interest rates pursued throughout the autumn. At the same time arrangements with the International Monetary Fund (IMF) were successfully concluded, and this led to expectations of increases in gilt-edged prices, thus greatly stimulating sales of government securities to the public. Government accounts were in surplus in December and futher surpluses were expected for seasonal reasons (tax payments in January–March). The authorities considered that these influences would impose heavy pressure on bank reserves, leading to acute stringency in the money market and causing interest rates to rise. The authorities did not wish to see a rise in interest rates: in November and December 1976 the combination of interest levels in the UK and abroad and of the forward discount on sterling made the principal interest rate differentials be moderately against the UK, thus discouraging inward capital movements without encouraging outward movements. The improvement in confidence following the conclusion of the agreement with the IMF caused the forward discount on sterling to decline; in the absence of major changes in foreign interest rates, the preservation of 'competitive' relationships between UK and foreign rates required that UK rates should fall, or at least that they should not rise.

On 13 January 1977 the Bank of England announced that special deposits equivalent to 1 per cent of eligible liabilities would be released to banks and finance houses on 17 January; on 27 January a further release of special deposits (1 per cent of eligible liabilities) was made, but on this occasion the authorities stated that the release was temporary, to be re-lodged with the Bank of England on 10 March 1977. The Bank of England made it clear that special deposits were released to ease the conditions in the money market, and that this action did not indicate relaxation of the official policy stance.

The release of special deposits had a quick and pronounced effect on short-term interest rates. Between 14 and 28 January interest rates in the discount market fell by about $1\frac{1}{2}$ per cent, bringing the minimum lending rate down from 14 to $12\frac{1}{4}$ per cent; in the parallel money markets principal rates fell rather more sharply; e.g., the rate on sterling CDs decreased by over 2 per cent. These changes contrast with near stability of rates in parallel money markets throughout November and December. (In the discount market Bank of England tactics caused interest rates to decline very gradually but steadily from their peaks at the end of October 1976.) Rates fell again between 28 January and 4 February and then remained fairly stable until the beginning of March.

The release of special deposits on 17 January 1977 amounted to about £700 million, and enabled the banks to balance a large part of the seasonal decrease in deposits and reserves owing to the net flow of funds from the private sector to the government. Not only were the banks able to absorb repayment of some £900 million of central government debt without suffering a reserve strain; bank reserves rose between reporting dates in December 1976 and January 1977 by about £100 million and the combined reserve ratio went up from 13·8 to 14·4 per cent. This improvement in the banks' reserve position and the fact that they increased their loans to discount houses (mainly in replacement of maturing Treasury bills), which the latter used to acquire a wide range of sterling money market assets, were the principal factors that eased the situation in the market and caused a general fall in interest rates.

The (temporary) release of special deposits on 27 January 1977 affected conditions in the money market in a similar manner. On this occasion (in the month to mid-February) the release of special deposits approximately balanced the repayment of government debt to the banking sector, i.e. enabled the banks to finance their customers' net payments to the government without losing reserves. At the same time, however, eligible liabilities were declining (partly as a result of net payments by bank customers to the government) and the banks were willing to reduce their reserve ratios. These influences eased the reserve position, and the banks felt able to reduce their holdings of reserve assets and replace them by higher-yielding liquid assets not having reserve status. They acquired these assets (non-reserve loans to the discount market, non-reserve bills, sterling CDs, etc.) mainly from discount houses, and the houses used funds so obtained to pay off their debts to the Bank of England. As a result of these operations conditions in the money market were eased as desired by the authorities.

It appears legitimate to conclude that releases of special deposits in January 1977 were effective in affecting money market conditions and that their use strengthened official influence over short-term interest rates.

Special Deposits as a Smoothing Device

The introduction of supplementary special deposits endowed the authorities with an instrument for restraining the growth of bank lending by limiting their willingness to acquire loanable resources. Thus, the authoritities found themselves able to use ordinary special deposits for short-period manipulation of the banks' reserve position. The object of such manipulation is to ease the reserve position when it is, or is expected to be, under temporary strain and to tighten it again when the strain has disappeared. The authorities achieve these aims by simultaneously announcing a release of special deposits equivalent to a stated proportion of eligible liabilities and the date at which the same proportion of eligible liabilities must be lodged again with the Bank of England. The first operation of this type took place in January 1977 (referred to at the end of the preceding section); temporary releases of special deposits were also made in June, July and August 1978.

The authorities vary special deposits for smoothing purposes not out of concern for the banks' reserve position as such but to prevent transient changes in reserve position from forcing the banks to undertake operations that would have undesirable effects on the monetary situation – particularly on interests rates. A significant tightening of the reserve position, if unrelieved, tends to induce the banks to bid for funds in parallel money markets and/or to withdraw funds previously placed there. As a result interest rates tend to rise and, since rates in various markets are affected differently, a distortion of the structure of rates is likely to result. And an easing of the reserve position tends to induce bank operations that cause a fall in interest rates. Temporary fluctuations in interest rates are regarded by the authorities as disruptive, and that is why they act to prevent conditions that are likely to give rise to them.

Variations in special deposits for smoothing purposes can be regarded as measures supplementing orthodox operations in the money market – purchases and sales of Treasury, local authority and commercial bills by the Bank of England. They have the advantage of being unambiguously temporary in character and leave no rooom for a misunderstanding of the authorities' intentions. Another advantage is that releases of special deposits enable the banks to buy (or not to sell) short-term assets, and the banks are left free to decide what specific assets to buy – this enables the banks to purchase assets most suitable given each bank's needs, preferences and special circumstances, with the result that market effects are widely diffused. The banks' asset choices are, however, likely to be influenced by the length of the period for which special deposits have been released.

The temporary release of special deposits on 27 January 1977 and their re-lodgement on 10 March eased market conditions in February, when major repayment of government debt to the banks tended to make them unduly stringent, and prevented market rates from falling too fast and too far in March, when a substantial net inflow of reserves to the banks would otherwise have caused market conditions to ease sharply.

In June and July 1978 the reserve position of the banks came under considerable pressure owing to a combination of circumstances, among them large official sales of gilt-edged stocks to the public and seasonal growth of the note circulation. The authorities themselves pushed interest rates up by raising the minimum lending rate[8] on 8 June but did not wish them to increase further. Market conditions, however, were stringent, and the pressure on bank reserves was an important cause of that stringency. To supplement its orthodox operations in the market the Bank of England announced on 15 June that special deposits equivalent to $1\frac{1}{2}$ per cent of eligible liabilities would be released on 19 June but that the banks would be required to re-lodge them with the Bank: $\frac{1}{2}$ per cent on 3 July and 1 per cent on 24 July (later postponed to 11 September). Interest rates in the discount market and in the parallel markets did not fall significantly and, indeed, later in July there were indications of a tendency to rise. Another release of special deposits (1 per cent of eligible liabilities) was announced on 27 July and made on 31 July, the banks being required to re-lodge them on 26 September, and on 14 August special deposits amounting to £207 million were released to London and Scottish clearing banks because these banks' commitments to provide fixed rate export and shipbuilding finance made their position with respect to supplementary special deposits unduly difficult.[9] These releases of special deposits caused money market conditions to ease, and market interest rates declined.

In the months to mid-September and mid-October 1978 the central government and the rest of the public sector borrowed substantial amounts from the banking sector, causing a flow of reserves to the banks. The re-lodgements of special deposits on 11 and 26 September (equivalent to 1 per cent of eligible liabilities on each occasion) prevented the reserve position from becoming unduly easy. Interest rates eased slightly in the early part of September in both the discount market and in parallel money markets but acquired a clear rising tendency in the second half of the month; this tendency continued in October. Recalls of special deposits contributed a little to this movement of interest rates, though other influences – increases in US and Eurodollar rates and expectations of a more restrictive monetary stance – were probably more important.

As in 1977, short-period variations of special deposits were a useful additional policy instrument for influencing market interest rates.

CHAPTER EIGHT

Supplementary Special Deposits ('the Corset')

The Scheme

The supplementary special deposits scheme (described above – see pp. 41–2) was introduced in December 1973 to strengthen the ability of the authorities to restrain the expansion of bank and finance house credit and to make the imposition of such restraint less dependent on increases in interest rates.

The central and crucial feature of the scheme is that it subjects to a penalty any bank[1] or finance house that allows its interest-bearing eligible liabilities (IBELs) to exceed the officially determined 'permitted' level.

A bank or finance house that finds itself in this situation is required to place a fraction of the excess with the Bank of England as a non-interest-bearing supplementary special deposit. The fact that a fraction of resources obtained by a bank or finance house at interest must be held in the form of an asset not bearing interest is the penal aspect of the scheme. The magnitude of the fraction of excess IBELs that must be deposited – the rate of supplementary special deposits – depends on the size of the excess of IBELs outstanding over the permitted level: thus, the greater the excess of IBELs, the heavier the penalty. The effect of the supplementary special deposits scheme is to restrain the growth of IBELs by making it unprofitable for the banks to expand IBELs, in excess of the officially determined 'permitted' growth of this category of bank liabilities.

The British monetary authorities had never before attempted to regulate the banks' (and finance houses') liabilities. Thus, when the scheme was introduced in December 1973 it represented a considerable innovation in the technique of monetary control. It was the response of the authorities to changes in operational techniques and practices of UK banks, particularly changes in banking methods made by the clearing banks after 1971, that reduced the effectiveness of the instruments of control on which the authorities used to rely. Widespread adoption of the practice of liability management (see chapter 2 above) was particularly important among these developments. Under this system the banks plan the rate of acquisition of assets, particularly the rate of expansion of loans and advances for some time ahead; if the normal inflow of resources proves inadequate to provide for the planned acquisition of assets, the banks act to attract resources, mainly by increasing interest rates to suppliers of funds. The supplementary special deposits scheme was introduced to deter the banks from attracting resources in this manner and, by implication, to compel them to scale down their plans for expansion of loans and other assets so as to bring that expansion into sounder relationship with probable availability of resources.

The authorities decided to apply control of the banks' and finance houses' liabilities to one broad category of eligible liabilities (as defined at the introduction of competition and credit control arrangements in 1971), namely the interest-bearing component of eligible liabilities. The authorities' decision in this respect can be explained on two grounds. In the first place, interest-bearing liabilities are much more easily controllable by individual banks than those not bearing interest. The inflows and outflows of sight deposits (current accounts) into or out of individual banks depend much more on the action of the banking system as a whole and of the monetary authorities than on steps taken by individual banks. Thus, it would be both unfair and, probably, ineffective to penalize individual banks if their liabilities in this category expanded more than the authorities considered appropriate. On the other hand, the banks can – at least to some extent – control the growth of their interest-bearing liabilities. They can do so by increasing or decreasing interest rates they offer to suppliers of funds in relation to rates obtainable on other comparable assets. Second, the supplementary special deposits scheme was introduced to control marginal increases of bank resources because, of course, it is such marginal increases that may give rise to *excessive* expansion of bank (and finance house) lending. By their very nature marginal increases in resources, i.e. increases that are attracted by deliberate action of the banks, are all interest-bearing: for the purpose of this type of control the choice of IBELs was clearly appropriate.

The Working of the Supplementary Special Deposits System

The *modus operandi* of 'the corset' has three important aspects. (1) It is a device for curbing bank and finance house lending by making 'excess' lending unprofitable.[2] (2) By making 'excess' lending unprofitable it deters the banks from bidding for deposits and consequently prevents changes in the level and structure of interest rates which would induce the flow of funds to the banking system and would also have the effect of increasing the reserve base of the banking system, enabling and encouraging it to undertake multiple expansion of credit. Thus, the use of the 'corset' restrains the growth of the stock of money (sterling M3). (3) It reduces the demand for funds in the market and consequently tends to lower, or to prevent increases in, interest rates. Each of these aspects of the working of the supplementary special deposits scheme must be examined in some detail.

The banks operate for profit. Profits arise out of the excess of revenue generated by the use of resources (acquisition and holding of assets) over the cost of these resources. An additional 'unit of resources' can be profitably employed as long as the increase in the total cost of resources, i.e. the marginal cost of resources (which includes interest paid to suppliers of that unit of funds and upward adjustment in interest on other funds), is lower than the increase in revenue generated by the holding of assets, i.e. the marginal revenue. Both marginal cost and marginal revenue can be expressed as a rate per cent. Given the general structure of interest rates, the marginal cost of resources increases as the total volume of resources (liabilities) of a bank increases and the marginal revenue tends to decrease as the total of that bank's assets grows. Thus, the optimum – profit-maximizing – size of a bank's balance sheet is that at which marginal cost and marginal revenue are equal.

The obligation to place supplementary special deposits in respect of an additional unit of resources (IBELs) means that a fraction of that unit of resources must be balanced by an asset that bears no interest. In other words, the imposition of 'the corset' leaves the marginal cost of the relevant resources (IBELs in excess of a bank's target) unchanged but reduces the marginal revenue. Thus, the obligation to place supplementary special deposits reduces the optimum volume of liabilities (=assets) of every institution subject to that obligation. Consequently, it damps down the banks' and finance houses' desire to acquire additional resources and to expand loans.

A bank that actively tries to acquire additional resources indicates by doing so that it considers its actual size to be smaller than its optimum size, i.e. that its marginal revenue is significantly higher than its marginal cost. The fact that the imposition of 'the corset' reduces a bank's optimum size may not stop it from trying to increase its actual size. To have this effect 'the corset' must reduce marginal revenue to, or below, marginal cost at the actual volume of the liabilities (=assets) of the bank in question. The effectiveness of supplementary special deposits in deterring the banks from trying to acquire additional resources (IBELs), and thus in curbing bank lending, depends on their rate (the fraction of additional IBELs that must be placed with the Bank of England at zero yield).

Marginal costs of resources and prospective marginal revenues from assets are, of course, not the same for all banks. But they, and the margin between them, are unlikely to differ considerably because the principal factors governing them – interest rates payable in wholesale money markets and bank lending rates respectively – are common to all banks. Thus, the impact of the obligation to place supplementary special deposits at a certain rate or rates, while not identical on all banks, is most likely to be very similar.

The obligation to place supplementary special deposits in respect of a 'unit of liabilities' reduces the revenue from the balancing 'unit of assets'[3] because it forces the banks to include in the 'unit' zero-yielding supplementary special deposits instead of high interest-bearing assets. The proportion of supplementary special deposits in a 'unit of assets' is equal to the rate at which they are placed, which also shows the magnitude of the reduction in the proportion of other assets in the unit, these other assets being very largely high-yielding loans.[4] The decrease in the yield of a 'unit of assets' owing to the substitution in it of supplementary special deposits for loans is given by the product of the rate of supplementary special deposits and the yield of the displaced loans.[5]

In the absence of supplementary special deposits the yield of a 'unit of assets' is somewhat lower than the yield of loans (approximated by the average of bank lending rates), but the difference between them must be small because loans are likely to account for 70–80 per cent of a (marginal) unit of assets. The CD rate can be taken as an approximation to the cost of a 'unit of resources' (IBELs). Consequently, the margin between the revenue from a 'unit of assets' and the cost of a 'unit of resources' (IBELs) is likely to be a little narrower than the margin between the average of bank lending rates and the CD rate. The latter margin varies considerably, but it tends to be narrower than usual when the banks compete keenly for deposits – and it is in that situation that 'the corset' is likely to be operative. Thus, the 5 per cent rate of supplementary special deposits may be sufficient to reduce the revenue from assets below the cost of resources needed to hold those assets, but in some circumstances it may fail to do so. But there can be no doubt that the 25 per cent rate – and, of course, the 50 per cent rate – must make unprofitable loans on the basis of additional IBELs attracting supplementary special deposits at these rates. Consequently, supplementary special deposits curb bank lending and deter the banks from over-expanding their IBELs.

The foregoing analysis rests on the assumption that the banks' behaviour is profit-maximizing in the strict and simple sense that they aim at equalizing (increasing) marginal costs and (decreasing) marginal revenues. At times, however, the banks deviate from this simple rule. This may be fully rational, because the revenue from a loan (interest earned) may not fully reflect the advantages that the making of that loan can reasonably be expected to generate. For example, a loan made 'now' may be a means of establishing a new connection likely to bring in substantial new business – and therefore profits – in the future. Similarly, the desire to preserve the goodwill of important customers may constitute a powerful incentive to lend at current ruling rates even if funds for such lending cannot be obtained on terms that would make such loans directly profitable. Loans in fulfilment of commitments previously made cannot, of course, be refused, even though the cost of the necessary funds exceeds the previously agreed loan rates. More generally, a bank wishing to enter a new market or to develop a new type of business may well be prepared to sacrifice profitability in the short run for the sake of expected long-run advantages and profits. In cases of this type the relationship between marginal revenue and marginal cost may well be considered unimportant, and then the expected response to a change in this relationship may not occur. These, however, are 'special cases'. Ordinary, day-to-day business, which accounts for the bulk of the loans made by most banks, does not raise special problems; in most cases the attractiveness or otherwise of creditworthy loan projects can be adequately assessed by comparing the cost of the necessary funds and the prospective revenue from their use, that is to say by applying the strict rule of profit-maximizing behaviour broadly and flexibly interpreted. The assumption of profit maximization, which underlies the theoretical analysis of the banks' reactions to the imposition upon them of the obligation to place supplementary special deposits, does not cast doubts on the validity in practice of the conclusion drawn from that analysis.

To appreciate the general monetary significance of 'the corset' it is necessary to bear in mind the effects of interbank competition for deposits and other resources. These effects and the ways in which they come about were fully described and explained in chapter 2 (pp. 25–30 above). Very briefly, interbank competition for deposits tends to raise interest rates offered by the banks in relation to public sector debt, making term deposits with banks and CDs more attractive to holders than Treasury bills and short-dated government securities. The banking sector increases its resources (deposits balanced by holdings of reserve assets or assets easily convertible into reserve assets) because the banks' success in retaining or attracting private sector deposits forces the government to adjust its financing in such a way that new bank deposits are created and reserve assets flow to the banks. The increase in deposits is an increase in the stock of money, and the rise in reserves, which is at least its partial counterpart, provides a base for further monetary expansion. If the increase in the attractiveness of deposits with UK banks causes an inflow of foreign funds, the crucial effect is the decrease in the ability of the EEA to provide finance to the Exchequer which, again, forces the government to alter its financing so as to cause creation of new deposits and, consequently, an increase in the supply of reserve assets to the banks.

By effectively discouraging the banks from acting to attract additional deposits and other resources, the device of supplementary special deposits prevents the occurrence of the monetary effects specified in the preceding paragraph. Thus, 'the corset' is more than an instrument for damping down bank and finance house lending by making 'marginal' loans unprofitable; it is a truly monetary instrument which can be used to restrain general monetary expansion, whether that expansion is due to excessive interbank competition for deposits or to other pressures and tendencies in the system augmenting the resources of the banking system.

Bank Operations to Reduce IBELs and their Effects

When 'the corset' was introduced for the first time in December 1973, the target level of IBELs was set at a somewhat higher figure than the banks' aggregate IBELs reported for December 1973. The banks had to reduce the rate of growth of IBELs, but they did not need to reduce the absolute level of that category of liabilities, though in fact they did so. But when the scheme was re-activated in November 1976 the authorities imposed more stringent conditions such that to avoid the obligation to place supplementary special deposits the banks had to reduce IBELs substantially below their level in November 1976. Similarly, a substantial absolute decrease in IBELs was required of the banks when the scheme was re-activated again in June 1978.

The development of the official practice suggests that 'the corset' must be treated as a device that normally forces the banks to take measures to reduce the level of IBELs outstanding to bring it to the target level. Thereafter IBELs may be allowed to grow and the task of the banks is to maintain appropriate restraint on their rate of growth. This, however, requires that the creation of new IBELs should be largely balanced by the liquidation of existing ones, and the appropriate rate of liquidation is very likely to necessitate deliberate action on the part of the banks to dispose of some IBELs continuously. Broadly speaking, the same methods and instruments are suitable whether the aim of operations is an absolute reduction in the level of IBELs or a damping down of their rate of growth by discouragement of creation of new IBELs and by operations aimed at the disposal of existing ones.

The simplest and the most obvious measure to reduce the level, or the rate of growth, of IBELs is a reduction in interest rates offered by the banks on CDs and wholesale conventional term deposits, together, perhaps, with the easing of conditions on which the latter can be withdrawn before the agreed maturity date. The immediate effect is a fall in new issues of CDs and in placements of funds on deposit with banks, but as time goes on and existing term deposits mature these are likely to be increasingly withdrawn.

Funds not placed with or withdrawn from the banks seek investment in other assets[6] – new issues of public sector debt, temporary (market) loans to local authorities, loans to discount houses, private sector debt, e.g. inter-company loans, commercial bills, etc. The general effect of this change in the structure of supply of funds is a fall in interest rates in all the markets involved. But the change in the structure of the flow of funds affects the structure of bank liabilities.

Purchases of new issues of public sector debt or lending to deficit units in the private sector transfer funds to borrowers who use the funds so acquired to finance spending. Bank deposits of the recipients of these outlays increase; in the first instance all these deposits are current accounts and many of them are likely to remain in this form. To that extent, what were, or would be, the banks' IBELs are transformed into non-interest-bearing liabilities (NIBELs). It must also be noted that the use of funds not placed with, or withdrawn from, the banks to buy new issues of public sector debt reduces public sector borrowing from the banking sector and, consequently, the flow of reserves to the banks.

Increases in non-bank temporary lending to UK local authorities have a different significance. The funds so put at the disposal of the local authorities are likely to be largely used not to finance spending but to reduce the local authorities' indebtedness to the banks. As a result, interest-bearing deposits withdrawn from the banks, or current account deposits which would otherwise be turned into interest-bearing ones, are extinguished, balancing the decrease in the banks' assets (loans to local authorities). An equal decrease in deposits and non-reserve assets strengthens the banks' reserve position and the banks can make new loans, equal in amount to the repayment of loans by the local authorities; new deposits are generated, and at least some of them are likely to retain the form of current account deposits. The banks' IBELs decrease, but if the banks fully utilize their lending capacity, the fall in IBELs reflects their transformation into NIBELs and not a fall in the volume of resources in the hands of the banks.

Generally speaking, increases in non-bank lending to discount houses enable the houses to increase purchases of both public and private sector debt.[7] In this case the effects on the banks' IBELs are the same as those of direct use of funds withdrawn from, or not placed with, banks to buy public or private sector debt described above. But increases in non-bank lending to discount houses may also play a very important part in other arrangements made by banks to reduce IBELs and/or to maintain the flow of credit to their customers.

It should be borne in mind that in calculating eligible liabilities (total or interest-bearing) a bank's holdings of certificates of deposit (issued by other banks) are deducted from its own issues. Thus, the banks can reduce the level of IBELs outstanding by buying CDs from non-bank sellers, in most cases from discount houses. From the banks' point of view these operations raise the problem that in order to pay for the CDs bought they must cancel some of the money at call with the discount market, thus reducing their own reserves. This limits the magnitude of the CD-buying operations, but the limitation may not in fact be very serious: as time goes on more and more non-reserve bank loans to discount houses mature and the proceeds can be immediately re-lent at call, thus rebuilding holdings of reserve assets. From the point of view of the discount houses sales of CDs to the banks raise the problem that both their liabilities and assets decrease. Increases in non-bank lending to discount houses help solve this problem by providing replacement for funds no longer supplied by the banks. Discount houses can then use these funds to rebuild their holdings of high-yielding undefined assets to replace CDs sold to the banks. The banks are likely to be instrumental in generating the supply of such assets (commercial bills) by accepting bills on behalf of their customers instead of lending to them.[8]

Purchases of CDs by banks reduce IBELs outstanding. They also tend to reduce interest rates in the secondary market for CDs, because the banks must bid up their prices; other discount market rates may also be adjusted downwards. But taking purchases of CDs in conjunction with other operations connected with them, it is clear that the resulting fall in IBELs does not cause a parallel contraction in the flow of lending (bank and non-bank) to the private sector. Nor does it cause a decrease in the flow of reserve assets to the banks. Thus, these operations constitute action to avoid the pressures imposed by 'the corset' rather than a channel through which these pressures are transmitted to the real sector of the economy.

Individual banks can cause a fall in their IBELs by reducing the volume of interbank deposits taken. They can effect this reduction by lowering interest rates offered in the interbank market. If all (or most) banks take such action, a very sharp fall in interbank interest rates may result. While individual banks can suceed in reducing IBELs in this way, aggregate IBELs cannot be decreased by operations in deposits of banks with banks. This is because a decrease in the volume of interbank deposits taken must be balanced by a fall in interbank deposits placed, and these, like holdings of CDs, can be deducted in computing each bank's eligible liabilities. Banks are likely to be differently placed with respect to the IBELs target; some may be able and willing to let their IBELs rise. In such a case interbank operations can facilitate the reduction of IBELs by banks that must achieve it. But the counterpart of a net reduction of a bank's IBELs in the form of interbank deposits must be a loss by that bank of an equal amount of reserve assets.[9]

As a result of the various operations undertaken by the banks in order to reduce their IBELs, interest rates in virtually all organized financial markets are likely to fall. A general fall in market rates is virtually certain to cause the banks to lower their base rates and, consequently, their lending rates on the one hand and rates paid on seven-day retail deposits on the other.[10] Building society rates and rates charged by HP companies may also be affected.

The instrument of supplementary special deposits is unique among monetary instruments in that it exerts downward pressure on both the rate of growth of the stock of money and on interest rates. Thus, the instrument raises hopes that the achievement of a given degree of restraint on the rate of monetary growth may be compatible with a lower level of interest rates than would be possible if the authorities relied on the more usual instruments – open-market operations or (ordinary) special deposits. The lower level of interest rates has advantages and disadvantages. It can facilitate the maintenance of a sound relationship between interest rates at home and abroad and can thus ease the problem of possible distortions and difficulties arising from international capital flows; it can prevent increases in politically sensitive rates, e.g. mortgage rates; it reduces the budget cost of national debt service and the balance of payments cost of service of foreign held debt. On the other hand, the rate of interest is the principal means of transmitting monetary pressure to the real sector; 'the corset' weakens this role of interest rates because by restraining the rise, or causing a fall, in lending rates it lessens the incentive to cut down the demand for loans. This makes it more difficult for the banks and others to reduce the volume of lending, and the achievement of the cut in bank lending desired by the authorities may require the application of some form of bank credit rationing. And this may severely distort the allocation of financial resources and cause inefficiency in their use.

The foregoing examination of bank operations to reduce IBELs shows that these operations induce a measure of disintermediation in the financial system. Instead of placing their (short-term) funds with the banks and leaving them to allocate these funds to the various, competing, final uses, the suppliers of funds lend directly to the users of funds. The market for financial resources becomes more segmented and consequently more imperfect. As a result, the allocation of financial resources is likely to become further removed from the theoretical optimum allocation. In practice, the significance of disintermediation in the present context is unlikely to be very great. The suppliers of wholesale funds who shift them from placement with the banking system to more direct investment are financial institutions and large industrial and commercial companies; they operate in the same financial markets as the banks, and there seems little reason to think that the quality of allocation of financial resources through organized financial markets is likely to be adversely affected by disintermediation. But the banks lend to a very extensive range of customers who do not have access to financial markets, whereas other financial institutions and non-financial companies tend to specialize in lending. It is in this connection that disintermediation may give rise to adverse effects in that financial resources may not be supplied to some would-be users, not because the uses in question are genuinely less worthwhile than others, but merely as a result of institutional influences. It must be borne in mind, however, that if the funds circulate within the private sector the banks do not lose resources and their capacity to lend remains unimpaired. It is only if funds not placed with, or withdrawn from, the banking system are supplied to the government that the generation of bank deposits and the flow of reserves to the banks are reduced, forcing the banks to restrict lending. But this is the result of the absorption of resources by the government rather than of disintermediation as such.

The Effects of Supplementary Special Deposits, 1974–80[11]

It is clear that in the periods July 1974–February 1975, May–July 1977 and November 1978–November 1979, 'the corset' scheme induced most of the banks and finance houses to arrange their business so as not to exceed the penalty-free level of IBELs. The largest number of institutions that placed supplementary special deposits in any one of the 24 relevant months was 14 (out of about 360 institutions subject to the scheme) in July 1974 and in August 1979, and the largest total amount placed was £10 million in August 1979, when the penalty-free level of IBELs was about £33,000 million. But between November 1979 and July 1980 the impending termination of 'the corset' scheme reduced the incentive to banks to keep IBELs within penalty-free limits; in May 1980 28 institutions placed supplementary special deposits totalling £219 million, and in July 1980 47 institutions placed £456 million.

The effects of supplementary special deposits can be examined in a more meaningful way by observing changes in the rates of growth of various aggregates between periods relevant to the operation of 'the corset' scheme. Three such relevant periods can be distinguished in relation to each activation of the scheme: (1) the pre-activation period, viz. six months preceding the activation of the scheme; (2) the adjustment period, viz. the period between the activation of the scheme and the time when the obligation to place supplementary special deposits becomes operative; (3) 'the corset' period, viz. the period during which supplementary special deposits must be placed in respect of excess IBELs.

Table 4 shows rates of growth of the principal categories of bank liabilities, reserves and the stock of money in the three periods mentioned above.[12] The pattern of changes in these growth rates is not identical on the three occasions when 'the corset' was imposed, but there is sufficient similarity to permit fairly confident conclusions.

The figures show clearly that the activation of the supplementary special deposits scheme is followed by a sharp reduction in the growth rate of IBELs (particularly in the adjustment period), while the growth rate of NIBELs tends to increase;[13] the growth of total eligible liabilities also decreases – this reflects the fact that IBELs account for about two-thirds of the total. The behaviour of the rate of growth of M3, or sterling M3, is similar to that of the growth rate of IBELs, but changes are, naturally, less sharp. Moreover, differences between rates of growth of M1 and M3 (or sterling M3) tend to diminish considerably. The rate of growth of the banks' holdings of eligible reserve assets tends to decrease sharply – in fact, to become negative – in the adjustment period, but to rise sharply in 'the corset' period. In short, the behaviour of these

TABLE 4 *Annual Rates of Growth of Some Monetary Aggregates*

	IBELs	NIBELs	Eligible liabilities	Eligible reserve assets	M1 unadjusted	M1 seasonal. adjusted	M3 [a] unadjusted	M3 [a] seasonal. adjusted
	%	%	%	%	%	%	%	%
Pre-activation period June 1973–Dec. 1973	–	–	36	28	1·5	−2	35·5	34
Oct. 1973–Dec. 1973	37·5 [b]	19 [b]	29	28	16·5	9	31	26
Adjustment period Dec. 1973–June 1974	0·8	−4	0	−3	−2	0·8	7	8
'Corset' period June 1974–Feb. 1975	7·5	13	9	8·5	11	16	12	12
Pre-activation period May–Nov. 1976	31·5	3·5	22	2·5	12·5 [c]	11·5	16·5	15
Adjustment period Nov. 1976–Apr. 1977	−18	14·5	−9	−5	11	11	−2	−1
'Corset' period Apr. 1977–July 1977	11·5	21·5	14·5	9·5	17·5	19·5	13·5	12
Pre-activation period Nov. 1977–May 1978	29	10	22·5	4·5	18	19·5	18	21
Adjustment period May 1978–Oct. 1978	−9	21·5	0	−11	12·5	11·5	8·5	8
'Corset' period Oct. 1978–Oct. 1979	15	14	14	13	13·5	13·5	13	13·5
Oct. 1979–June 1980	27	−4·5	15·5	13·5	−4·5	−5	9·5	10

[a] M3 between June 1973 and Feb. 1975; sterling M3 from May 1976. [b] Data for IBELs and NIBELs not available before October 1973. [c] This rate is much higher than that of NIBELs because of sharp increases in the growth of currency in circulation and of interest bearing sight deposits.

Source: Calculated from statistics in the *Bank of England Quarterly Bulletin*, Statistical Annex, March 1974, June 1974, September 1975, March 1977, June 1977, September 1977, June 1978, December 1978, June 1979, December 1979; Financial Statistics August 1980.

aggregates appears to be broadly as indicated by the analysis of the effects of supplementary special deposits.

It must be noted that the data shown in table 4 probably exaggerate the effectiveness of supplementary special deposits. In the view of the Committee of the London Clearing Bankers,[14] monetary growth would have declined in the first half of 1974 even if 'the corset' had not been imposed. This was likely partly because banking expansion in the preceding six months had been inflated by precautionary borrowing induced by fears that stringent restrictions would be imposed, partly by overdraft/CD arbitrage owing to distortions in the pattern of interest rates etc. and partly because political and other influences in the early months of 1974 tended to damp down expansionary tendencies in the economy. More specifically, private sector demand for bank credit was not strong throughout 1974 and public sector borrowing from the banking sector was significantly lower in 1974 than it had been in 1973. Thus, declines in the rate of growth of IBELs and of total eligible liabilities, and consequently in the rate of monetary growth, were due in part to general economic and financial influences and only partly to the effects of supplementary special deposits.

Between November 1976 and April 1977 the demand for bank credit was weak and consequently bank lending to the private sector was small,[15] and during the first quarter of 1977 the public sector repaid debt to the banking sector. In other words, influences independent of 'the corset' tended to damp down the growth of eligible liabilities and bank reserves and thus the rate of monetary growth. But the decline in IBELs while the growth of NIBELs accelerated – reflected in the disparity of behaviour of M1 and sterling M3 – suggests that supplementary special deposits exerted significant pressure. The authorities evidently considered that the rate of monetary growth after April 1977 was satisfactory: the operation of the supplementary special deposits scheme was suspended early in August 1977 although it had been intended to keep it operative until the end of the year.

During the adjustment period from May to October 1978 the banks succeeded in reducing their IBELs quite sharply, but this was roughly balanced by the growth of NIBELs, so that eligible liabilities as a whole remained virtually unchanged. These changes in bank liabilities were reflected in a sharp fall in the rate of growth of sterling M3 and a less sharp but significant deceleration of the growth of M1. It seems likely that supplementary special deposits were important in bringing about these changes. But between October 1978 and October 1979 monetary growth again proceeded at higher rates, with sterling M3, seasonally adjusted, growing faster than the target rate published in October 1978 and even more so than the target rate announced in June 1979. At the end of 1979 and in the early months of 1980 IBELs grew very fast. The rate of monetary growth decreased somewhat, but this was a reflection of a fall in NIBELs and not an effect of 'the corset'.

Table 5 presents some information about the effects of 'the corset' on bank lending.[16] Clearly, the activation of the supplementary special deposits scheme reduces the rate of growth of bank advances, but equally clearly, the effect is strongly influenced by the state of demand for bank loans. The dramatic decrease in the growth rate of advances between the periods May–November 1976 and November 1976–April 1977 was not repeated between November 1977–May 1978 and May–October 1978 because in the last mentioned period the demand for credit was not significantly weaker than in the preceding six months. Moreover, when demand for credit is strong, while the banks are forced to restrain lending they tend to increase the volume of acceptances thus passing actual lending on to discount houses[17] and to other suppliers of funds to whom bills accepted by banks are close and often attractive substitutes for CDs. It is also worth noting that, when the growth of their eligible liabilities is constrained, the banks tend to increase, sharply, the proportion of accretions of resources (eligible liabilities) used to give advances to customers. It follows that supplementary special deposits cause the banks to alter the structure of their assets. This reduces the effect of the restraint of IBELs on bank lending.

When the supplementary special deposits scheme was introduced in December 1973 interest rates were high (partly owing to increases induced by the calls for ordinary special deposits which had been made shortly before) and there were anomalies in the structure of rates. From January 1974 until February 1975, i.e. throughout the period during which the banks were subject to 'the corset' interest rates followed a steady downward trend. Principal money market and short-term gilt-edged rates at the beginning and end of that period are shown in table 6. Operations that the banks undertook to dispose of IBELs and to slow down the creation of new IBELs were an important influence causing interest rates to fall, especially during the first half of 1974. But there were at that time more general influences, domestic and external, which

TABLE 5 *Behaviour of Bank Advances and Acceptances*

	Annual rate of growth of bank sterling advances		Annual rate of growth of sterling acceptances by banks	Increase in advances as % of increase in eligible liabilities	
	to UK residents	to UK private sector		Sterling advances to UK residents	Sterling advances to UK private sector
	%	%	%	%	%
Pre-activation period June 1973–Dec. 1973	42·5	n.a.	48	75·5	n.a.
Adjustment period Dec. 1973–June 1974	16	n.a.	52·5	[a]	n.a.
'Corset' period June 1974–Feb. 1975	13	n.a.	32·5	102·5	n.a.
Pre-activation period May 1976–Nov. 1976	23	21·5	12	70	64·5
Adjustment period Nov. 1976–Apr. 1977	2	3·5	3	[b]	[b]
'Corset' period Apr. 1977–July 1977	23·5	23	36·5	110	106·5
Pre-activation period Nov. 1977–May 1978	18·5	18	−10	56	53·5
Adjustment period May 1978–Oct. 1978	15·5	13·5	169·5	[c]	[c]
'Corset' period Oct. 1978–Oct. 1979	22	22	65	108	104
Oct. 1979–June 1980	22	21	28·5	105	97·5

[a] Advances rose while the rise in eligible liabilities was negligible.
[b] Advances rose while eligible liabilities fell.
[c] Advances rose while the rise in eligible liabilities was negligible.

Source: Calculated from statistics in the *Bank of England Quarterly Bulletin*, Statistical Annex, March 1974, September 1974, September 1975, March 1977, September 1977, September 1978, December 1978, June 1979, December 1979; Financial Statistics, August 1980.

TABLE 6

	Treasury bills (average discount rate on allotment)	London clearing banks' base rate	Sterling certificates of deposit (3 months)	Short dated (5 years) gilt-edged stocks (redemption yield)
	%	%	%	%
End-Dec. 1973	12·42	13	15⅞	12·50
Mid-Feb. 1975	9·80	11½	11 1/16	11·21

Source: Bank of England Quarterly Bulletin, March 1974 and March 1975 (reproduced with the Bank's permission).

tended to make the monetary situation less tight and which therefore exerted a steady downward pressure on interest rates. It must be noted that the downward trend of rates continued after the supplementary special deposits scheme was suspended.

At the time of reactivation of 'the corset' in mid-November 1976, interest rates were again very high, though they had passed their peak two or three weeks earlier. As in 1973–74 interest rates declined steadily throughout the period during which the banks were subject to 'the corset' – at the beginning and end of that period the rates are shown in table 7. Again, as in the previous case, operations that the banks had

TABLE 7

	Treasury bills (average discount rate on allotment)	London clearing banks' base rate	Sterling CDs (3 months)	Short-dated gilt-edged stocks (redemption yield)
	%	%	%	%
Mid-Nov. 1976	14·00	14	14 7/16	14·60
End-July 1977	7·30	8½	7⅝	10·27

Source: Bank of England Quarterly Bulletin, December 1976 and September 1977 (reproduced with the Bank's permission).

to undertake to reduce IBELs were a contributory cause of the fall in interest rates, especially during the early part of the period, but the slackness of the demand for credit and the decline in interest rates abroad exerted more important downward pressures on interest rates. Because of these general influences interest rates continued to fall after the operation of the supplementary special deposits scheme was suspended early in August 1977.

The supplementary special deposits scheme was reactivated again in June 1978 as part of a package of measures including the raising of the minimum lending rate.[18] The initial reaction of money market rates was an upward adjustment which induced London clearing banks to increase their base rates by 1 per cent (to 10 per cent). Thereafter, however, the Treasury bill rate (average rate on allotment) drifted down continuously until October, but the three months' interbank rate and the CD rate (three months) remained somewhat higher than before the imposition of measures of restraint until the end of July, and although they eased a little later they did not become significantly lower than at the beginning of June. Thus, virtually throughout the 'adjustment period' interest rates did not fall as they had done on the two previous occasions when 'the corset' was imposed on the banks. These movements of interest rates were largely due to two influences. (1) The demand for credit was strong and this made it difficult for the banks to take action to reduce IBELs. (2) Large sales of gilt-edged stocks to the non-bank private sector imposed pressure on the banks' reserve position – this stimulated demand in the interbank market and caused interbank rates to rise while keen bidding for Treasury bills reduced rates on them.

Between October 1978 and February 1979 short-term interest rates were rising steadily. This movement was set off by a sharp increase in the minimum lending rate – an official act designed to stimulate sales of gilt-edged stocks so as to damp down the growth of the stock of money – but in the early months of 1979 it was strengthened by uncertainties about the general economic position and expectations of a further raising of the minimum lending rate. A change in market views and expectations caused an easing of interest rates in March 1979 and this was consolidated by two reductions in the minimum lending rate. Table 8 indicates the character of interest rate movements between June 1978 and May 1979.

The foregoing, very brief, review of the principal effects of 'the corset'

TABLE 8

	Treasury bills (average discount rate on allotment)	London clearing banks' base rate	Sterling CDs (3 months)	Short-dated (5 years) gilt-edged stocks (redemption yield)
	%	%	%	%
Beginning of				
June 1978	8·77	9	$9\frac{9}{16}$	11·55 [a]
Mid-June 1978	9·13	10	$9\frac{13}{16}$	11·47
End Sept. 1978	9·17	10	$9\frac{9}{16}$	12·14
Mid-Nov. 1978	11·73	$12\frac{1}{2}$	$12\frac{7}{32}$	13·00
Mid-Feb. 1979	12·70	$13\frac{1}{2}$	$13\frac{9}{16}$	13·22
End May 1979	11·45	12	$11\frac{13}{16}$	11·23

[a] 31 May

Source: Bank of England Quarterly Bulletin, December 1978 and June 1979 (reproduced with the Bank's permission).

suggests that the imposition on the banks of the obligation to place supplementary special deposits in respect of excess IBELs reduces the rate at which the banks' IBELs and total eligible liabilities grow and therefore damps down the rate of monetary growth; it suggests also that the impact of that obligation on bank lending depends to a considerable extent on the strength of the demand for bank credit, being weaker if the demand for credit remains strong; it suggests, finally, that the scheme exerts only a limited influence on interest rates, easily outweighed by more general market factors and, of course, by official management of interest rates.

CHAPTER NINE

Competition and Credit Control – An Appraisal

The Nature of the Competition and Credit Control System

The competition and credit control system was devised after a thorough review by the authorities of the principles and techniques of monetary management used in the 1950s and 1960s. The conclusion that the authorities appear to have drawn from that review was that, not only were the monetary techniques employed inadequate and fraught with disadvantages, but also, the approach to monetary control during the relevant period was based on an inadequate theoretical model of the transmission mechanism.

In the 1950s and 1960s the British financial system was riddled with cartel arrangements, artificial distinctions and barriers; consequently it was not a competitive system. Once it was decided actively to promote competition in the financial system, it became necessary to adopt a model of the transmission mechanism appropriate to the competitive nature of the financial environment.

In a competitive system – given investors' preferences, attitude to risks, expectations, etc. – demands for assets and their supplies are governed by the structure of relative asset yields. Investors strive to maintain utility-maximizing portfolios and to this end engage in portfolio adjustment operations in response to changes in all relevant influences, changes in relative yields being the most obvious and often the most important. Yields of financial assets are determined in the markets in which they are traded by means of normal market processes: excess demands or supplies of assets pushing yields down or up to the levels at which markets clear. But expected yields of real assets depend on their replacement costs and on the estimated values of the streams of services they are expected to produce over their useful lives. The difference in the ways in which yields of financial and real assets are determined is a very important feature of the working of the mechanism that transmits monetary impulses to the real sector of the economy.

The authorities can affect demand-and-supply conditions in financial markets by their own operations in these markets (purchases or sales of securities) or by forcing or inducing the banks to undertake operations in response to pressure imposed on them by official action (e.g. special deposits). The immediate effects of these operations are changes in yields of the assets in question, but the consequent alterations in relative yields bring about, very quickly, sympathetic changes in yields of an increasingly wide range of financial assets. Thus, official action causes yields of financial assets generally to rise or to fall. But expected yields of real assets are not affected at this stage, so that the relationship between yields of financial and of real assets alters in favour of the former or of the latter respectively. In other words, if official action causes interest rates to rise, the relative attractiveness of holding real assets decreases and this damps down the willingness of economic units to hold real capital.* In an economy in which net investment is normally positive, this damping down of the willingness to hold real capital reveals itself in a decrease in the investment component of aggregate demand. When this occurs the deflationary monetary impulse has been transmitted to the real sector.

In the abstract, a decrease in the willingness to hold real assets is usually taken to imply an increase in the willingness to hold financial assets. In practice, it is more likely to have its counterpart in a decrease in the desire to add to liabilities, i.e. in a decrease in the demand for loans.

The examination of the structure and working of competition and credit control arrangements strongly suggests that the authors of the

* This point can also be expressed by saying that a rise (or fall) in yields of financial assets increases (or decreases) the rate of discount used in calculating present values of streams of services of capital goods, causing a reduction (or increase) in the values placed on capital goods by their holders or prospective holders. These values are demand prices for capital goods. Supply prices being unchanged, a fall in demand prices results in a decrease in demand for real assets.

scheme visualized the transmission mechanism of the kind just sketched out. This explains the importance that the authorities attach to interest rate effects of measures of monetary policy, particularly the effect on bank lending rates. It also explains why reserve arrangements were adopted that did not endow the authorities with the ability to control firmly the supply of reserve assets to the banking system: changes in the reserve position as such were considered to be of secondary importance, relevant only in so far as they caused the banks to undertake operations in financial markets resulting in changes in interest rates.

Competition and credit control arrangements were designed with due regard to the structure and operational characteristics of the financial system in its modern form, but, given these arrangements, the nature of adjustment processes following official policy action is in substance the same as that envisaged by the traditional theory of monetary control. The rate of interest is the centrepiece of the system in the sense that all effective adjustments are brought about by changes in the level and structure of interest rates; official operations – open market sales or purchases of bills and bonds, calls for and releases of special deposits – are vitally important because they induce changes in interest rates rather than as instruments independent of (or alternative to) the rate of interest.[1]

Another important traditional feature of the competition and credit control system is that adjustment processes under it are entirely market processes, i.e. processes consisting of responses and reactions of economic units – the banks and the public – to changes in economic incentives engineered by official action. It follows that the efficiency of the competition and credit control system, i.e. the ease, smoothness and speed with which these arrangements make possible the accomplishment of the desired adjustment (a change in the rate of monetary growth[2]), depends on the strength and promptness of responses of economic units to changes in their circumstances and in the relevant interest rates.

Discussing the competition and credit control scheme in an address to the International Banking Conference in Munich in May 1971, the then Governor of the Bank of England said:

> It is not expected that the mechanism of the minimum asset ratio and Special Deposits can be used to achieve some precise multiple contraction or expansion of bank assets. Rather the intention is to use our control over liquidity,

> which these instruments will reinforce, to influence the structure of interest rates. The resulting changes in relative rates of return will then induce shifts in the asset portfolios of both the banks and the public.[3]

These matters were discussed in considerable detail in chapter 6, and it was pointed out that the most important among these portfolio adjustments were changes in the volume, or in the rate of growth, of bank advances (assets of the banks, liabilities of the public) and the corresponding changes in bank deposits (liabilities of the banks, assets of the public). This has two important implications.

In the first place, it may give rise to the question whether in devising the scheme its authors intended to provide the authorities with the means of implementing a bank and finance house credit policy or a truly general monetary policy. The quantitative importance of changes in bank advances in relation to changes in other bank assets as counterparts of changes in the total volume of bank deposits may suggest that the former interpretation is correct. This is not so. Under the competition and credit control system the principal instrument of adjustment is the rate of interest. The effects of changes in the level and structure of interest rates are far wider than their impact on bank and finance house lending. These changes affect the demand for public sector debt and therefore public sector borrowing from the non-bank private sector and from the banking sector; and this, in turn, affects the flow of eligible reserve assets to the banks. Moreover, changes in interest rates affect people's willingness to hold asset money balances – a rise in rates tends to induce holders of such balances to exchange some of them for other assets. If the rise in interest rates is general, asset balances are likely to be used by their owners to acquire a wide range of assets, among them assets currently issued by the public sector and assets disposed of by the banks. In the former case public sector borrowing from the banks is reduced so that new deposits are not created and the supply of reserve assets to the banks is curtailed. In the latter case deposits decrease and so do the banks' non-reserve assets. In short, changes in interest rates tend to affect the reserve position of the banking system and therefore its ability to acquire assets, not only during the adjustment process but also after that process has been completed. It follows from the foregoing that competition and credit control arrangements enable the authorities to generate a general and pervasive monetary pressure and not merely to increase or lighten pressure on bank and finance house lending. The fact that any change in the volume or rate of growth of bank deposits must be balanced largely by a corresponding change in bank advances is merely a reflection of the high proportion of advances in the total of the banks' non-reserve assets.

The second implication relates to very fundamental issues. A rise in interest rates (specifically in bank lending rates)* causes the volume of advances to the private sector to fall, or the rate of growth of advances to decline, because it damps down the *demand* for bank credit. But a contraction in the demand for bank credit, whether it takes the form of a fall in the volume of new borrowing or an increase in the volume of repayments, reflects a downward revision of spending plans of the economic units concerned. In other words, it reflects the fact that the rise in the cost of finance owing to increases in bank lending rates has reduced expected profitability of economic activities financed by bank loans – e.g. acquisition and holding of stocks of materials and finished goods, work in progress etc. – making some of them unattractive and therefore inducing a reduction in their volume; thus, outlays that would have been made, e.g. to increase the volume of stocks held or to increase the rate of production (reflected in a rise in work in progress) etc., are not made, and therefore funds need not be borrowed from the banks; and if stocks are run down or if the scale of operations is reduced, current inflows of funds that would have been needed to finance current outlays become available for repayment of advances. If the contraction of the demand for bank credit is such that the current flow of loan repayments exceeds current lending (so that there is an absolute decrease in the volume of bank advances outstanding), there is a net flow of deposits from the private sector to the banks; other things being the same, the cancellation of these deposits results in a decrease in the total volume of bank deposits that balances the fall in advances outstanding. If the contraction in the demand for credit reduces the excess of current new lending over the current flow of loan repayments but leaves it positive, there is a decrease in the rate of growth of advances and, other things being the same, a decrease in the rate of creation of new deposits and consequently in the rate of growth of the stock of money.

It follows from the foregoing that, to the extent that the fall in the

* It should be noted that in the speech already quoted the Governor of the Bank of England said: 'no limitation is envisaged on the authorities' ability . . . to bring about sufficiently strong pressure on bank lending rates'; O'Brien, 'Key Issues', p. 197 (reproduced with the Bank's permission).

stock of money, or a decrease in its rate of growth, results from the contraction in the demand for bank credit induced by a rise in bank lending rates, it is the consequence and *not* the cause of private sector economic units' decisions that result in a decrease in the flow of total private spending, or in the rate of growth of private sector spending.[4] The causal sequence of adjustment under the competition and credit control regime is as follows:

– pressure on reserves imposed by special deposits forces the banks to undertake operations that *cause* market rates of interest to increase;
– increases in market rates *cause* the banks to raise lending rates (via base rates or directly);
– increases in lending rates reduce the profitability of economic activities and *cause* some existing activities to be scaled down and some planned activities not to be undertaken so that private sector spending decreases;
– the decrease in private sector spending reduces the amount of bank credit needed by the private sector and thus *causes* a decrease in net bank lending, the counterpart of which is a fall in the rate of creation of new deposits (and therefore a fall in the rate of growth of the stock of money) or, if net bank lending is made negative, a fall in the volume of bank deposits (and therefore a fall in the stock of money).

Bank operations in the money and gilt-edged markets and the effects of these operations (increases in interest rates) can induce private sector owners of funds to use them to acquire assets disposed of by the banks or supplied by the authorities instead of to lend to the private sector.

In the former case funds withheld or withdrawn from private sector borrowers are surrendered to the banks and the deposits in which they are embodied are cancelled, i.e. the stock of money is reduced. This decrease in the stock of money is a direct counterpart of the reduction in the availability of funds to private sector deficit economic units. These units, as a group, curtail plans to expand their economic activities, or even their actual activities; they do this not because these activities have become unattractive but because of lack of the necessary finance. The curtailment of economic activities causes a reduction in the planned expansion of private sector spending and may cause actual spending to be cut down. This reduction in private sector spending is the consequence of operations (use of loanable funds to buy financial assets from the banks), one aspect of which is the reduction in the stock of money.

In the latter case funds are withheld from deficit economic units in the private sector and made available to the government. The effects of this diversion of funds on private sector spending are the same as those described in the preceding paragraph. The availability of their funds to the government enables it to reduce *pro tanto* its borrowing from the banking sector, with the consequence that new bank deposits are not generated; i.e., an increase in the stock of money or in its rate of growth is prevented or damped down.

It must be noted, however, that both in the former case and in the latter the ultimate cause of all adjustments is the rise in interest rates.

The Supply of Money and the Demand for it

Some of the problems discussed in the preceding section can also be usefully considered from the standpoint of the relationship between changes in money supply and in the demand for money.

A reduction in the stock of money means that some units of money are cancelled, and it follows that in order to reduce the stock of money it is necessary to cause economic units to surrender money balances to the banks for cancellation.[5] In view of the market orientation of the competition and credit control system, economic units must be induced to surrender their money balances by ordinary economic incentives, deposits being surrendered either in exchange for assets disposed of by the banks or in discharge of debts to the banks. Money holdings of economic units are reduced owing to deliberate decisions of the holders taken as a result of increases in interest rates. Thus, these reductions reflect the contraction of the demand for money brought about by rises in interest rates, and it follows that control over the supply of money is exercised by influencing the demand for it.

It is very important to bear in mind that the bulk of any change in the stock of money is the counterpart of the corresponding change in the total of bank advances. Because of this a decrease in the stock of money is, largely, a decrease in the active part of the money stock, the part that is being used and re-used in making current payments. This occurs because those who have decided to repay bank advances use the proceeds of current sales to do so instead of using them to make payments for goods and services. The decrease in the flow of payments made by some economic units reduces the flow of money receipts of other economic units. The latter must contract their payments, but for obvious reasons they try to minimize this contraction by drawing on money balances to make payments that cannot be financed out of current receipts. The average level of these balances – mainly transactions balances but possibly some precautionary ones – is reduced; the lower level of balances can be maintained because of the decrease in the volume of business (receipts and payments).[6]

It follows from the foregoing that net repayment of bank advances has two important effects: (1) it reduces the rate of flow of aggregate demand and therefore of the money national income; (2) it makes economic units other than those repaying bank loans reduce their money balances; i.e., it brings about a diffused reduction in the demand for money in line with the fall in the national money income. A symmetrical argument applies to the case of action to increase the stock of money.

The aim of restrictive monetary policy is usually to reduce the rate of growth of the stock of money rather than to cause an absolute reduction in the stock of money itself. The damping down of the demand for bank loans restrains the growth of aggregate demand (and of the money national income) and consequently reduces the desire of economic units to add to their money balances. The decrease in the rate of growth of the stock of money goes *pari passu* with the decrease in the growth of the demand for money.

It is important to observe that in the absence of a decrease in the demand for money the effectiveness of a reduction in bank lending (by means, perhaps, of official controls) in causing a fall in the rate of growth of the stock of money is likely to be limited and uncertain. Desiring to increase their money holdings but unable to do so by acquiring bank deposits generated by net bank lending, economic units are virtually certain to resort to other ways of building up money balances, e.g. reducing purchases of new issues of government debt or selling off holdings of government debt approaching maturity to the authorities. These operations force the government to increase borrowing from the banking sector; the resulting creation of new deposits offsets to some extent the effects of the restriction of bank lending on the rate of growth of the stock of money. The importance of this factor varies according to circumstances, but it is often likely to be very considerable. Thus, to accomplish desired changes in the stock of money and its rate of growth the authorities must take steps to influence the demand for money.

The authors of the competition and credit control scheme cannot be criticized for taking the relationship between the demand for and the supply of money to be crucial for the exercise of monetary control. It is less clear that they can escape criticism for making the influence over the demand for money virtually the only channel through which to control the supply of money (see p. 138 below).

The authorities can influence the demand for money by varying interest rates, and thus the principal problem in this connection is that of the interest elasticity of the demand for money function. The higher the numerical value of this elasticity, the larger is the change in the aggregate desired holdings of money in response to a given change in the relevant interest rate or rates.

At the time when the competition and credit control scheme was being drawn up, Bank of England's estimates of the long-run interest elasticity of the demand for money fuction were:[7] for the M1 definition of money, −1·05 with respect to the short-term rate of interest and −0·80 with respect to the long-term rate; for the M3 definition of money, −0·21 and −0·51 respectively. These estimates suggested that practicable changes in interest rates, e.g. increases by one or two percentage points, would cause significant changes in the aggregate desired holdings of money by the public.[8] Thus, it could be expected that only moderate increases in interest rates would be needed to restrain the growth of the demand for money sufficiently to prevent unwanted increases in the stock of money. In fact, however, the Bank of England had to cause or allow more than 'moderate' increases in interest rates on several occasions during the 1970s, and even so it is not clear that it was always successful in keeping the growth of the stock of money on target.

Interest Rates and the Stock of Money

The discussion in the preceding two sections highlights the fact that under competition and credit control arrangements the rate of interest governs the process of monetary adjustment. Virtually all changes, reactions and responses that constitute this process are brought about by movements of interest rates. Moreover, changes in the stock of money or in the rate of its growth are, in large measure, consequences of changes in aggregate demand due, directly or indirectly, to changes in the demand for real assets caused by changes in interest rates. Since the aim of monetary policy, within a wider framework of economic policy, is to influence the rate of flow of aggregate demand, it appears to follow from the above that the rate of interest should be the direct object of monetary policy, the stock of money being left to adjust itself to the level and structure of interest rates that ensure that aggregate demand flows at the desired level and grows from year to year at the desired rate. In fact, however, there are several problems and complications.

The rate of growth of aggregate demand is more closely and more consistently (though not precisely) related to the rate of growth of the stock of money than to the rate of interest. Thus, it is possible to determine the rate, or a range of rates, of monetary growth that reflects, approximately, the desired rate of growth of aggregate demand; measures taken in order to make the stock of money grow at the rate so determined cause changes in interest rates which tend to ensure that the actual rate of growth of aggregate demand is not substantially different from the desired rate.

A full analysis of the monetary requirements and implications of continuous growth of the national output is outside the scope of the present study. But the principal issues should be noted.

(1) The productive potential of a growing economy increases from year to year and thus its continuous full utilization implies growing aggregate supply of goods and services.
(2) Absorption of growing aggregate supply requires that aggregate demand should also grow from year to year so as to be equal to aggregate supply at the desired level of prices.
(3) Therefore, spending on currently produced goods and services financed, directly or indirectly, out of the current national income must be regularly supplemented by spending financed out of increases in the stock of money.
(4) The rate at which the stock of money must increase from year to year to provide for the necessary growth of aggregate demand (target rate of monetary growth) depends on the potential rate of growth of aggregate supply, changes in the demand for money and

the desired (or acceptable) rise in the price level (if any); it can be determined on the basis of forecasts of these three factors. (In practice, allowance must be made for external factors – balance of payments deficit reduces the increase in the money stock needed to support a given increase in aggregate demand).

(5) The principal determinant of the actual rate of growth of the stock of money is the level of net bank lending or, at one remove, the growth of the banks' lending capacity. If the growth of lending capacity is greater than is consistent with the target rate of growth of aggregate demand, interest rates tend to fall. The cheapening of bank credit generates a desire to increase aggregate demand and the availability of finance makes it practicable to increase it; consequently, the growth of aggregate demand exceeds that of aggregate supply and prices rise. If the growth of the banks' lending capacity is smaller than is consistent with the target rate of growth of aggregate demand, interest rates rise and the actual growth of aggregate demand is insufficient to ensure full absorption of aggregate supply; some unemployment of resources results.

On the other hand, the relationship between the level and structure of interest rates and aggregate demand is very variable, and consequently attempts to determine in advance 'the rate of interest' consistent with the equilibrium level of aggregate demand in a given period would be subject to a very considerable margin of error; furthermore, 'the target rate of interest' would need to be altered, probably substantially, from period to period to make aggregate demand grow in line with the growth of aggregate supply. In other words, the rate of growth of the stock of money provides a more reliable and more stable monetary target than the rate of interest.

At the time of the introduction of the competition and credit control system the importance of controlling the growth of monetary aggregates (stock of money, domestic credit expansion, etc.) was strongly emphasized, but there was no mention of making the rate of growth of one of these aggregates an explicit target of monetary policy. The rate of growth of the stock of money was given this status in July 1976 when 12 per cent was stated to be the target rate of growth of M3 for the financial year 1976–77 (in December 1976 it was replaced by a target range of 9–13 per cent).

The question that must now be considered is whether or not competition and credit control arrangements constitute an appropriate framework for the policy of controlling the rate of growth of the stock of money so as to keep it within target range.

It was demonstrated in chapters 4 and 5 that official control over the flow of reserve assets to the banks is virtually always imperfect and at times very limited indeed. This greatly impairs the ability of the authorities to influence the lending capacity of the banking system, with the result that the growth of bank lending is virtually demand-determined. Consequently, bank lending can be restrained only by a rise in bank lending rates sufficient to damp down the demand for bank loans. But if the banks' reserve position does not seriously limit their ability to lend, the banks have no incentive to increase lending rates *in order* to reduce the demand for loans; they adjust lending rates (via base rates or directly), but only to preserve margins over the cost of loanable funds to them. Thus, for bank lending rates to rise to the point at which they effectively discourage the demand for loans, increases in money market interest rates must first take place. This raises two problems. First, among the market interest rates that rise are rates offered by the banks on wholesale deposits; it was explained in chapters 2 and 8 that this can increase the flow of funds to the banking system and thus strengthen the banks' reserve position and augment their lending capacity. Second, a widespread, sharp rise in interest rates has well-known disadvantages and often tends to give rise to conflict of objectives and policies. When such conflicts arise compromise solutions are usually adopted, and these inevitably involve an easing of the rate of interest pressure, which, of course, weakens the impact of policy on the stock of money.

If the authorities could exercise firm control over the flow of reserves to the banking system they would be able to restrain the growth of the banks' lending capacity; this would force the banks to take action to limit their lending irrespective of the demand for loans. Given the market orientation of the system, this action would take the form of increases in lending rates, increases sufficiently sharp to bring down the demand for loans to equality with their available supply. The rise in bank lending rates needed to bring about a given measure of restraint of bank lending would be approximately the same as under the present system, but since movements of bank lending rates would depend less on changes in market rates of interest increases in the latter could and probably would be smaller.

The ability of the authorities to restrain bank lending was improved by the introduction of the supplementary special deposits in December 1973 because the imposition of 'the corset' reduces the banks' willingness to expand lending. But it remains inadequate, because the authorities' control over the lending capacity of the banking system is weak and uncertain.

An important implication of the imperfection of official control over the flow of reserves to the banking system is that the authorities cannot exercise a continuous influence over the growth of the stock of money so as to prevent the occurrence of substantial deviations from the target rate of growth.[9] They cannot do so because they have no means of regulating current acquisitions of reserve assets by the banks. Thus, monetary control is exercised by taking measures to correct deviations that have already occurred. Unavoidably, there is a recognition lag, owing to delays in obtaining information reliable enough to constitute a basis for policy decisions, and a lag between the taking of monetary measures and the appearance of their effects. The policy of *ex post* correction of observed deviations has the result of producing short-term variations in the actual rate of monetary growth, which, if substantial, tend to be disruptive and damaging.

It follows from the above that, if objectives of monetary policy are formulated in terms of target rates of growth of the stock of money, their effective pursuit requires that the authorities should be able to exercise a stronger and more certain control over the supply of reserves to the banks than they can do under competition and credit control arrangements. This suggests that cash – the supply of which the authorities can control – should be the only reserve asset of the banks and that the authorities should supply it without penalty only to the extent that the amounts supplied were consistent with the target rate of growth of the stock of money. It must be noted that the operation of such a system (as indeed of any 'monetary base' control) would not be simple and easy as a summary statement implies. Many problems would be involved, and some important structural changes in the monetary and financial framework might be necessary.[10] Interest rates would continue to play a fundamental part in such a control system because any restriction of the supply of cash would cause interest rates to rise and the rise in rates would restrain the acquisition of assets by the banks and thus the creation of bank deposits. But the rise in rates would tend to be consistent with the target rate of growth of the stock of money.

In view of the inability of the authorities to control firmly the reserve position of the banks, it is not surprising that the Bank of England has often sought to exert influence directly on interest rates.[11] Action of this kind is often necessary to strengthen and to speed up market tendencies. But the Bank of England has been criticized[12] for pursuing an active rate of interest policy in the sense of having (unstated) interest rate targets and taking steps to push rates to these targets. Quite clearly, such a policy is not consistent with the pursuit of stock of money objectives, however formulated, because, in R. S. Sayers's phrase,[13] it is 'one of the eternal verities' that interest rates and the supply of money cannot be simultaneously controlled independently of each other. Once a certain level and structure of interest rates has been established the stock of money must become what the market wishes to absorb at these rates, no more and no less, irrespective of any stock of money targets, whether published or not. And vice versa, actual stock of money can be equal to the target stock only if interest rates are allowed to move freely to the level and structure that induce absorption of just the target amount of money.

It is not practicable to pursue an active rate of interest policy in order to generate the desired rate of growth of the stock of money or the desired size of the money stock, because it is impossible to determine in advance the interest rates that would have these effects. The range of influences operating on the public's demand for money is very wide, and the impact of interest rates on these influences tends to vary from case to case; people's responses to changes in the influencing factors are also variable, and, moreover, all reactions and responses occur with variable time lags. There are also many relevant influences outside the field of the demand for money, e.g. external influences, in particular international capital flows. Accurate forecasting of all the relationships involved is beyond the bounds of possibility.

Supplementary Special Deposits

It was explained in chapter 8 that supplementary special deposits have two main effects: (1) they make the banks less willing to lend and therefore reduce bank lending to the private sector; (2) they divert some funds away from the banking sector and to the government. It follows that supplementary special deposits tend to reduce the availability of financial resources to the private sector and to increase their availability to the public sector. To the extent that this reallocation of financial resources occurs, supplementary special deposits operate as a device for crowding out private sector expenditure. The reallocation of financial resources takes place because, in order to keep their IBELs in line with the target imposed by the authorities, the banks must take action that so alters the structure of interest rates that some funds which, if interest rates were market determined, would be supplied to the private sector are supplied to the public sector.

It is important to note that an essential feature of the mechanism that brings about the reallocation of financial resources is the damping down of the banks' demand for deposits by restricting them to an officially imposed IBEL target made effective by severe financial penalties. Thus, a non-market pressure is introduced at one of the crucial points of the network of the flows of funds; necessarily, the structure of these flows changes and so does the allocation of funds to their uses. Moreover, the purpose of the limitation of the banks' demand for IBELs is to cause a fall in the supply of bank loans to the private sector, irrespective of the demand for these loans. In other words, the aim of supplementary special deposits is very similar to the aim of ceilings on bank lending used in the 1950s and 1960s. The drawbacks of the two methods are also similar.

When the competition and credit control system was introduced in 1971 one of the aims was declared to be to ensure that the allocation of financial resources was governed by the price mechanism, i.e. by market-determined interest rates, official operations being undertaken to influence general market conditions and not to put pressure on particular classes of financial transactions. In view of the effect of supplementary special deposits just described, and of the way in which this effect is brought about, it is clear that the use of this instrument constitutes a deviation from the aims and intentions of the system as originally conceived.

The central feature of the supplementary special deposits scheme is the target rate of growth of IBELs. This is uniform for all banks and finance houses subject to the scheme; that is to say, the maximum permitted rate of expansion of IBELs is the same for all of them. But the restriction so imposed on the growth of particular banks is not equally severe: on the contrary, it bears more heavily on the more efficient banks than on the less efficient ones. The former are prevented from undertaking profitable business and are thus deprived of the rewards of their efficiency; the latter may have their actual rate of expansion only slightly restricted, and in some cases there may be no restriction at all. Indeed, some lending business which the more efficient banks are prevented from undertaking may shift to the less efficient institutions, the fall in interbank interest rates enabling the latter to obtain the necessary lending resources by acquiring the former's surplus IBELs. The fact that the use of 'the corset' may result in support being given to the less efficient banks at the expanse of the more efficient ones is an obvious drawback of the scheme.[14] It also indicates that the supplementary special deposits scheme is inconsistent with the general economic aim of competition and credit control arrangements, viz. the promotion of efficiency in the working of the monetary system.

The clearing banks consider that 'the corset' puts them at a disadvantage *vis-à-vis* the non-clearing banks. This is due to some special features of the business of clearing banks. Their lending to customers is predominantly in the form of overdrafts, and therefore the volume of their lending fluctuates considerably as outstanding overdraft facilities are drawn upon by customers and, on the other hand, as existing overdrafts are reduced. These fluctuations are governed by the flows of receipts and payments of the banks' customers, and the banks cannot exercise control over them. Normally the clearing banks can finance sudden increases in lending by, for example, borrowing in the interbank market. But if the supplementary special deposits scheme is operative such borrowing may easily make a bank's IBELs exceed the penalty-free level. To avoid finding themselves in this situation the clearing banks must plan their lending so that the volume of IBELs needed to provide for it is substantially below the maximum officially permitted level. But if upsurges in the use of overdraft facilities do not take place, such cautious planning results in profitable business not being undertaken. The problem of fluctuations in the volume of overdraft lending by the clearing banks is compounded by their being in effect lenders of last resort to local authorities and financial institutions. Non-clearing banks often require these borrowers to repay loans on make-up days (reporting dates), and this forces the debtors to draw on their overdraft facilities or stand-by credit lines with the clearing banks. Thus, claims on clearing banks are passed to non-clearing banks and are used by them to increase their deposits with the clearing banks. As a result, non-clearing banks reduce their IBELs on reporting dates, but the clearing banks' IBELs increase. In other words, in some circumstances the non-clearing banks can shift their IBELs problems on to the clearing banks. The fact that 'the corset' has somewhat different effects on clearing and non-clearing banks respectively constitutes yet another deviation from the spirit of competition and credit control arrangements.

Whenever they activate the supplementary special deposits scheme, the authorities indicate that the exigencies of the current situation require and justify a temporary departure from the aims and principles of the competition and credit control system. Thus, the use of the scheme can be (and has been) described as a 'triumph of expediency over principle'.

The issue is very complicated, however. To impose monetary restraint by purely market means, interest rates must be allowed to rise, and with expected rates of inflation of the order of actual rates prevailing in the UK in the second half of the 1970s, the necessary rise in interest rates may be very considerable. This would be so even if the authorities could control the reserve position of the banking system much more firmly and decisively than they can do under competition and credit control arrangements. Under these arrangements, however, the banks have very wide scope for the practice of liability management; when liability management is practised on a large scale, and when private sector demand is strong, the effects of a rise in interest rates may have perverse effects, i.e. may stimulate monetary growth[15] instead of restraining it. Demand for bank credit is not perfectly interest-inelastic, and there must always be a level of interest rates high enough to reduce it sufficiently to restrain monetary growth. But this level may be so high as to be disruptive both internally and internationally.

At the end of 1973 the authorities decided that it was essential to devise an instrument that would enable them to restrain monetary growth without having to push interest rates intolerably high. Supplementary special deposits meet these requirements and thus have considerable advantages as a weapon of monetary management. It is arguable that these advantages outweigh the obvious and serious drawbacks of the instrument of supplementary special deposits.

Generality and Fairness of Competition and Credit Control Arrangements

Before 1971 only the London clearing banks maintained specified reserve (cash and liquid assets) ratios, and only they and the Scottish banks were required to place special deposits when called upon to do so. Non-clearing banks were free from these rules and obligations, though in the 1960s requests to limit lending were addressed to them in the same terms as to the clearing banks. By the end of the 1960s it was generally recognized that, in view of the increase in non-clearing banks' share in domestic banking business, the concentration of control on the clearing banks was no longer appropriate: the incompleteness of coverage impaired the effectiveness of monetary management, the differences in treatment generated anomalies, distortions and a feeling of unfairness among bankers.

Under the competition and credit control system the principal rules are uniformly applicable to all listed[16] banks and finance houses with only three exceptions: the minimum reserve ratio for finance houses is 10 per cent instead of $12\frac{1}{2}$ per cent as for the banks; only clearing banks are required to hold balances with the Bank of England amounting to $1\frac{1}{2}$ per cent of their eligible liabilities; and Northern Ireland banks are not required to place special deposits or supplementary special deposits.

London clearing banks have expressed the view that the obligation to hold zero-yield balances with the Bank of England discriminates against them because it makes the average yield of reserve assets held by them lower than that obtainable by the non-clearing banks. Moreover, the nature of their business forces the clearing banks to hold substantial amounts of notes and coin (a zero-yield, *non-reserve* asset), whereas non-clearing banks' holdings of vault cash are negligible.[17] The feeling of grievance experienced by the London clearing banks is understandable, but there is little real justification for it. The clearing banks need to hold both forms of cash because they operate the principal mechanism of payments in the economy and the performance of this function brings the clearing banks important benefits; in particular, non-interest-bearing current account deposits form a much higher proportion of total deposits of clearing banks than of non-clearing banks. Because of this, the average cost of resources is lower to the clearing banks, and this provides 'compensation' for the interest foregone owing to the need to hold cash.[18]

A more important and more complicated problem arises out of the fact that in the case of the clearing banks receipts and payments (other than transactions in currency at branch offices) take the form of additions to and drawings on their balances with the Bank of England, but in the case of non-clearing banks they consist of additions to and drawings on their working balances with London clearing banks. This is significant because balances with the Bank of England are reserve assets but balances with the clearing banks are not.[19]

If a clearing bank buys non-reserve assets it experiences a fall in reserves (but reserves of the banking system are unchanged), and if it acquires reserve assets, e.g. money at call or Treasury bills, its reserves remain unchanged (and the reserves of the system increase). If these transactions are undertaken by a non-clearing bank the former has no effect on that bank's reserves but the reserves of the clearing bank with which it holds working balances decrease (the reserves of the system are unchanged); the latter increases reserves of the non-clearing bank and again reduces reserves of its clearing bank (but reserves of the banking system increase). It appears that individually non-clearing banks are in an advantageous position relatively to clearing banks, but that this has no effect on the banking system as a whole. In fact, there is no genuine advantage on either side.

Apart from the banks' reserve-creating operations, new reserves flow to the banks mainly as a result of net government payments or of EEA's sterling payments for net purchases of foreign currencies. Recipients deposit cheques with their banks. If the bank with which these cheques have been deposited is a clearing bank, the presentation and settlement of cheques increases its balance with the Bank of England; if it is a non-clearing bank it passes these cheques to its clearing bank, increasing its working balances with it, and the clearing bank presents the cheques for settlement and increases its balance with the Bank of England. At this stage reserves of the non-clearing bank do not increase, although its customers have deposited with it claims on the Bank of England, but reserves of the clearing bank in question increase. The relative advantage that non-clearing banks appear to enjoy when they acquire assets merely constitutes the undoing of the apparent relative disadvantage that they suffer when reserves flow into the banking system.

Clearing and non-clearing banks compete for customers' deposits, and the question arises whether or not they compete on equal terms. If, in the course of interbank competition a clearing bank loses a deposit to another clearing bank, the result is a transfer of reserves (a balance with the Bank of England) from the deposit-losing bank to the deposit-gaining bank. The former then rearranges reserves to recover balances with the Bank of England and disposes of non-reserve assets to rebuild holdings of reserves, and the latter acquires non-reserve assets in substitution for surplus reserves.

If a clearing bank loses a deposit to a non-clearing bank whose working balance it holds the immediate effect on the deposit-losing bank is merely an increase in the non-clearing bank working balance and an equal decrease in a non-bank customer's deposit.* The deposit-gaining bank uses the increase in its working balance to buy reserve and non-reserve assets and it pays for them by passing claims on the deposit-losing clearing bank to asset-sellers. These claims are presented in most cases by other clearing banks – acting for themselves, or on behalf of their non-bank customers or other non-clearing banks – and the deposit-losing bank meets these claims by transferring balances with the Bank of England to other clearing banks. It then rearranges reserves and sells non-reserve assets as in the case of losing a deposit to another clearing bank.

If a non-clearing bank loses a deposit to a clearing bank that holds its working balance there are no immediate effects on eligible liabilities and on reserves of either bank. But non-clearing banks do not normally hold excess working balances, and so the deposit losing bank must make good the depletion of its working balance owing to the initial loss of a customer's deposit. To do so it must dispose of assets – partly reserve[20] and partly non-reserve assets – and deposit the proceeds, in the form of claims on clearing banks, with the clearing bank that holds the working balance (and which is also the deposit gaining bank). The latter experiences an equal increase in reserves and in elgible liabilities and this enables it to acquire non-reserve assets.

If a non-clearing bank loses a deposit to a clearing bank that does not hold its working balance, the effects on the deposit-losing bank are the same as in the preceding case. The deposit-gaining clearing bank is affected as it would be if it attracted a deposit from another clearing bank, and the clearing bank that holds the deposit-losing bank's working balance first experiences an outflow of reserves and then,

* If the deposit-losing clearing bank does not hold the deposit-gaining non-clearing bank's working balance, the effect on it is the same as if it lost a deposit to another clearing bank.

when the deposit-losing bank rebuilds its working balance, an inflow of reserves.

The effects of shifts of deposits from bank to bank are identical in substance irrespective of the group or groups to which the banks concerned belong. Competition and credit control arrangements ensure that all banks compete on equal terms, so that in this respect they satisfy the criterion of fairness between institutions to which they apply.

Operations of non-clearing banks, whether repayment of deposits or acquisition of assets, sometimes cause reserve losses to clearing banks that hold their working balances. But these reserve losses tend to be transient, because non-clearing banks normally rebuild working balances[21] very quickly. Even if non-clearing banks make a 'permanent' reduction in their working balances, the proceeds of their net payments (claims on clearing banks) must, with one exception, be redeposited with clearing banks, though of course not necessarily those that must meet the claims. The exception occurs if non-clearing banks buy assets from the authorities and the authorities use the proceeds not to make payments but, for example, to redeem Treasury bills held by the Banking Department of the Bank of England.[22] Thus, operations of non-clearing banks affect clearing banks in the same manner as do operations of non-bank customers. The fact that non-clearing banks are customers of clearing banks does not confer special advantages or impose burdens on either group of banks.

The London clearing banks consider that certain operations undertaken by non-clearing banks to reduce, or to restrain the growth, of IBELs so as to escape the obligation to place supplementary special deposits shift the burden of adjustment from non-clearing banks on to the clearing banks. These operations were outlined in the preceding section, and it appears that the clearing banks have a legitimate grievance in this respect. To escape this particular burden the clearing banks would need to discontinue the provision of stand-by credit facilities to local authorities, finance houses and, indeed, non-clearing banks. The discontinuation of these arrangements would undoubtedly be disadvantageous, but whenever the supplementary special deposits scheme is operative, they may expose clearing banks to pressure that in fairness should be borne by the non-clearing banks.

Competition and credit control arrangements apply to banks, finance houses, the discount market and (since October 1978) the National Giro. Other deposit-taking institutions – National and Trustee Savings

Banks and building societies – are outside the ambit of the scheme,[23] as are other financial institutions – insurance companies, pension funds, etc. Thus, the scheme is not fully general, but this defect is less serious than it might at first sight appear to be.

Savings banks collect small savings and channel them to the public sector by means of investment in government and local authority securities. Thus, on the lending side they do not compete with the banks, and there is no way in which their operations could stimulate private sector spending. On the deposits side, however, there *is* an element of competition with the banks.

Deposits with savings banks are an obvious substitute for bank deposits, especially, of course, current account deposits with Trustee Savings Banks. They are for all practical purposes as liquid and secure as deposits with banks, and offer the advantage of favourable fiscal treatment. The banks consider that these special advantages divert the flow of savings from them to savings banks and that since this diversion is partly caused by non-market influences the terms of competition are unfairly biased against them. There is probably a case in equity for offering privileged treatment to certain categories of small savings as such rather than to savings entrusted to particular institutions; such a reform could be combined with the extension of competition and credit control arrangements to cover Trustee Savings Banks.

It is unlikely that the present exclusion of savings banks from the ambit of monetary control significantly impairs the effectiveness of control. The potential monetary significance of savings banks lies not so much in the operations of these institutions but in the fact that deposits with them are a readily available reserve of purchasing power. But rules for the conduct of the business of financial institutions cannot regulate the conduct of their customers so as to prevent them from taking action that could have undesirable macroeconomic consequences.

Building societies are outside the scope of the control system and therefore their growth depends only on the demand for building society loans and on the availability of funds to meet this demand. When the demand for mortgage loans is strong and lending rates can be raised, building societies can obtain additional funds by increasing rates offered on shares and deposits and thus attracting deposits from banks.[24] The monetary effect of a flow of deposits from banks to building societies is an increase in the velocity of circulation: at least some deposits moved from banks to building societies would have remained idle if left with the banks but become active when they pass to building societies. The total volume of bank deposits does not decrease as a result of the shift of some of them to building societies except to the extent that the societies use a fraction of the receipts to buy Treasury bills and other securities from the authorities for reserve purposes. There is no decrease in the stock of money to offset the rise in the velocity of circulation. And the increase in lending by building societies tends, directly or indirectly, to increase the flow of aggregate demand. If the prevailing economic conditions make this undesirable, the authorities are forced to take or tighten restrictive monetary measures and the resulting pressure falls mainly on the banks.

The fact that building societies are outside the control system impairs, or at least can impair, its fairness and probably also its effectiveness. And the fact that building society interest rates are subject to some influences other than those of market conditions means that the allocation of financial resources between building societies, banks and other institutions is not entirely governed by the price mechanism.

Other financial institutions – insurance companies, pension funds, investment and unit trusts – can also undertake operations causing activation of idle balances. This can occur if these institutions sell gilt-edged securities from their portfolios to holders of idle balances and re-lend the proceeds to deficit units in the private sector. Increases in velocity of circulation arising from such operations are unlikely to be large, especially if interest rates and security prices are determined by market forces, because in such circumstances interest rate movements tend to reduce the attractiveness of asset-switching operations. In view of this it does not appear probable that the fact that competition and credit control arrangements do not apply in some form[25] to insurance companies, unit trusts, etc., impairs the effectiveness of monetary controls.

The issue of fairness of the system also arises in connection with the composition of the group of assets that rank as reserve assets. Some money market assets are eligible reserve assets of banks and finance houses while others are not. The reserve character of the former stimulates demand for them and causes their prices to rise relatively to other assets; in other words, the structure of yields of short-term assets is affected by reserve status given to some of them. This is perfectly natural and understandable: if there are two assets closely similar in maturity, security, marketability, etc., of which one has and the other has not the status of a reserve asset, clearly the former is more attractive to holders and this must be expected to make a somewhat lower yield of that asset acceptable to asset-buyers.

The problem of fairness arises because the acceptability of lower yields on reserve assets enables the issuers of these assets to borrow more cheaply than those who issue assets closely similar in other respects but lacking the reserve status. It follows that under competition and credit control arrangements the government (as issuer of Treasury bills) and the discount houses (as suppliers of money at call to the banks) are privileged borrowers.

Assuming that it is necessary to impose reserve requirements on the banks, it is clear that the government must be at least the chief supplier of reserve assets. The privileged borrowing situation that the government thus obtains can then be considered to constitute partial compensation for the burdens it must bear in the interests of effective monetary management, e.g. the budgetary consequences of deliberately engineered increases in interest rates. On the other hand, it is difficult to justify the privilege conferred on discount houses. The only service that they and they alone render is the regular tendering for the entire issue of Treasury bills. At one time it was an important service: it made it unnecessary for the government to seek residual finance from the Bank of England and thus limited the unplanned flow of cash to the banking system. Under present arrangements Treasury bills and money at call, which finances discount market's holdings of Treasury bills, are themselves reserve assets, and therefore the flow of Treasury bills to the banking sector is just as expansionary as the flow of cash. Moreover, if on a particular Friday the whole issue of Treasury bills was not tendered for and the government had to obtain funds from the Bank of England, the resulting build-up of the banks' cash holdings would promptly induce the banks and discount houses to buy Treasury bills from the Bank of England's market agent. The possible deficiency of demand for Treasury bills at tender would not give rise to important undesirable monetary consequences, but the absence of guaranteed demand for them would probably raise the cost of this class of government borrowing. The discontinuation of the practice of 'covering the tender' would, however, have an important effect: it would deprive the Bank of England of an important instrument which it now uses to influence interest rates in the money market. If the availability of this instrument is considered very important, and if the obligation to 'cover the tender' is considered essential to ensure its availability, then financial benefits derived by discount houses from their position as suppliers of eligible reserve assets can be treated as a reward to them for assuming that obligation.

Concluding Comment

The introduction of competition and credit control arrangements in 1971 undoubtedly improved the structural and operational quality of the British monetary system. Cartel agreements on interest rates and conventional links between interest rates were discontinued and the authorities ceased to provide automatic support for the gilt-edged market. Moreover, the system of officially imposed ceilings on bank lending to the private sector was abandoned, though the authorities have retained the right to give qualitative guidance to the banks. Finally, the obligation to observe minimum reserve ratios and to place special deposits (and, later, supplementary special deposits) became general applying to all banks[26] and the larger finance houses.

As a result of the 1971 reforms, competition among banks greatly increased: the banks now compete keenly both as takers of deposits and as suppliers of loans. This competition takes the form of, mainly, price competition; thus it tends to promote the flow of resources to the more efficient institutions and induces all institutions to improve their efficiency by eliminating wasteful and outdated practices and by means of financial innovation.

The competitive character of the system ensures that, as the authors of the competition and credit control scheme intended, market-determined interest rates govern the allocation of financial resources among uses to a much greater extent than was the case in the pre-1971 era. Thus, in its 'competition aspect' the scheme can be judged to have been a success.

From the point of view of monetary control the success of the scheme is more debatable. Table 9 shows that the rate of growth of the stock of money, whether M1 or M3, varied considerably from year to year and fluctuated very sharply from quarter to quarter in each year. Some variations in the rate of growth of the stock of money must, of course, be expected. Economic conditions change, and some changes constitute legitimate reasons for deliberately causing changes in the rate of

TABLE 9 *Rates of Growth of the Stock of Money per annum*

Financial year	M1 seasonally adjusted: Increase in the year	M1: Range of increases in quarters (annual rates) min.	M1: max.	Sterling M3 seasonally adjusted: Increase in the year	Sterling M3: Range of increases in quarters (annual rates) min.	Sterling M3: max.	Target rates of growth
	%	%	%	%	%	%	%
1972–73	9·8	6·1	18·3	24·6	n.a.		–
1973–74	3·3	–10·4	29·7	23·8	n.a.		–
1974–75	19·0	10·0	36·2	10·1	n.a.		–
1975–76	18·1	10·8	21·5	5·4	2·4	13·9	–
1976–77	10·2	–1·6	19·3	8·3	0·8	17·4	9–13
1977–78	22·8	15·6	30·6	14·5	9·1	19·7	9–13
1978–79	13·1	3·6	23·4	11·5	5·7	18·3	8–12
1979–80	6·8[a]	–3·2	15·2	12·9[a]	7·0	16·5	7–11

[a] Between mid-April 1979 and mid-April 1980 M1 and sterling M3 (seasonally adjusted) increased by 2·7% and 10·7% respectively (banking months series). See also pp. 122–3 of the June 1980 *Quarterly Bulletin*.

Source: Bank of England Quarterly Bulletin, March 1975, March 1977, March 1978, September 1979, June 1980, table 11·1, End-of-quarter series.

monetary growth or allowing them to occur. Moreover, there must be some flexibility in the monetary system to enable it to adjust the provision of credit to changes in the demand for it, and such adjustments tend to be reflected in alterations in the rate of monetary growth. But sharp swings in the rate of growth of the stock of money are clearly undesirable; sudden increases in it have inflationary consequences, and sudden decreases impose severe strains on the liquidity position of the private sector, particularly the company sector.

The 'monetary explosion' in 1972–73 and 1973–74 was contrary to the wishes of the authorities. It occurred because of the ineffectiveness of special deposits as a weapon of restraint and because increases in interest rates, although considerable, were not large enough to damp down monetary growth. The introduction of supplementary special deposits and the adoption by the government of a more stringent fiscal stance made possible sharp reductions in the rate of growth of sterling

M3 in 1974–75 and 1975–76. These sharp reductions were made necessary by the very high rate of monetary growth in 1972–73 and 1973–74. In other words, the severe restriction of monetary growth was a consequence of the 'correction-after-the-event' approach to monetary control, itself largely due to the inability of the authorities to restrain the flow of reserve assets to the banks. The availability of the instrument of supplementary special deposits alleviates this problem to some extent and thus enables the authorities to improve their control over monetary growth. But it must be borne in mind that 'the corset' scheme conflicts with the aims and principles which underlie competition and credit control arrangements.

Since 1976 the authorities set and published monetary targets expressed in terms of a range of growth rates for seasonally adjusted sterling M3. In 1976–77 the actual rate of growth of sterling M3 was below the lower limit of the target range; in 1977–78 it was above the upper limit of the range; but in 1978–79 the 11·5 per cent increase in sterling M3 was within the 8–12 per cent targets limits.

Under the competition and credit control system the authorities cannot control the growth of the stock of money firmly and precisely. The main structural reason for this is the fact that, because of the nature of assets that have been chosen as eligible reserve assets, the authorities cannot regulate the flow of reserves to the banks. To strengthen the ability of the authorities to control the rate of growth of the stock of money, the present provisions concerning bank reserves need to be radically reformed. It goes without saying that effective control of the stock of money requires that interest rates should be allowed to reach the level and structure consistent with the target level of the money stock.

Postscript

In March 1980 the Bank of England and the Treasury issued a Green Paper entitled *Monetary Control* (Cmnd 7858). In this document, the purpose of which is to provide a framework for consultations about possible changes in monetary control arrangements and methods, the authorities have outlined their views on many problems of monetary management, and in the light of these considerations they have proposed certain alterations in the present competition and credit control system.

The object of monetary control is unambiguously stated to be the control of the money supply over the medium term together with reasonable stability of the rate of monetary growth in the short term. Seasonally adjusted rate of growth of sterling M3 is to continue to be the principal target variable.

Monetary growth results from – and therefore depends on – bank lending to the public sector and bank lending to the private sector. Given fiscal policy that determines the public sector borrowing requirement[1], the authorities can influence the volume of bank lending to both sectors by appropriately manipulating short-term interest rates. Changes in these rates, through ordinary market responses, cause changes in gilt-edged rates over a wide maturity range and therefore influence private sector demand for government and local authority securities as well as for Treasury bills and other short-term public sector debt. Consequently, the volume of public sector borrowing from the banks is affected. Bank lending rates normally follow market rates of interest, and so manipulation of short-term interest rates affects private sector demand for bank credit and, therefore, the volume of bank lending to the private sector.

Theoretical considerations suggest that the effects of the manipulation of short-term interest rates tend to be 'in the right direction' from the point of view of monetary control: raising these interest rates tends to restrain monetary growth, lowering them stimulates it. In practice, however, there are many problems, complications and uncertainties. It is legitimate to infer from the discussion in the Green Paper that three issues are particularly important.

(1) A rise in interest rates necessarily involves a fall in prices of fixed interest securities. It follows that, if interest rates are expected to rise, would-be buyers of gilt-edged securities set capital losses implicit in these interest rate expectations against interest yields of these stocks in calculating prospective rates of return on investments in these securities. In such circumstances even exceptionally high interest yields may fail to attract demand – and if an observed increase in the level of interest rates generates expectations of further rises, the initial increase may induce a contraction of demand for gilt-edged securities rather than an expansion in it. This is very important from the point of view of monetary control, because expectations of increases in interest rates arise whenever investors take the view that the current rate of growth of sterling M3 is higher than consistent with the official monetary target. The resulting decrease in the demand for gilt-edged stocks tends to raise the rate of monetary growth still further. Thus, sharp temporary fluctuations in the rate of monetary growth occur which may themselves be disruptive and which may increase fluctuations in interest rates.[2] There is little that the authorities can do to influence investors' expectations, but if interest rates are altered promptly whenever sterling M3 moves off-course, and if the adjustment of rates is pushed rapidly to the level that the market believes is sufficient to put sterling M3 on-course, the main cause of changes in expectations is likely to disappear.

(2) A rise in short-term market interest rates induces the banks to raise rates they offer on deposits and CDs as well as their lending rates. To serve the purpose of monetary restraint a rise in interest rates must (among other effects) induce deposit holders to use them to buy assets supplied by the authorities and the banks. Thus, it is necessary that interest rates on deposits and CDs should rise less than the yields of assets substitutable for bank deposits. Such a change in the structure of rates may or may not occur according to circumstances. It seems,

however, that it is less likely to occur if interest rates are pushed up by methods that involve pressure on the banks' reserve position. Under modern conditions the banks often respond to reserve pressure by trying to attract deposits and so to induce an inflow of reserve assets rather than, more traditionally, by reducing holdings of non-reserve assets and deposits. Competition for deposits tends to push up rates offered on them; whereas, at the same time, bidding for Treasury bills and other reserve assets (many of which are substitutes for bank deposits) obstructs increases in their yields. In such a situation investors have no incentive to replace money balances in their portfolios by other assets.

It can be inferred from the Green Paper that the authorities take the view that excessive increases in deposit rates are considerably less likely to occur if reserve pressure is not imposed on the banks. They also take the view that the imposition of reserve pressure is not a necessary element of official action to raise short-term interest rates; increases in the minimum lending rate (since May 1978 an administered rate determined by the authorities) and operations in the money market are fully sufficient for this purpose.

(3) Problems and difficulties outlined above led to the introduction of the supplementary special deposits scheme in 1973. Under this scheme penalties were imposed on banks that over-expanded interest-bearing eligible liabilities. The scheme provided solutions to some problems but gave rise to others, the most important among the latter being the problem of disintermediation (and re-intermediation). Disintermediation can be defined as shifts of lending business from the banks to other institutions, shifts not reflecting changes in relative efficiency but owing to differences in imposed pressures under which institutions in each of these groups operate. Re-intermediation describes shifts of lending business in the opposite direction.

Disintermediation is very undesirable. It causes a decrease in the allocative efficiency of the financial system, it increases risks which must be borne by the ultimate providers of funds and – this is particularly important from the point of view of monetary control – it partly offsets the effects of whatever reduction of monetary growth has been achieved with the concomitant result that it reduces the significance of sterling M3 as a monetary indicator. This is so because the principal forms of disintermediation involve increases in the velocity of circulation.[3] The increase in the velocity of circulation partly nullifies the restraint exerted on aggregate demand by the reduction in the rate of growth of sterling M3.

It is clear from the Green Paper that the authorities are not in favour of adopting a monetary base control system. There appear to be four main reasons for their attitude.

(1) Even in the case of a very rigorous monetary base control system, changes in the total volume of bank deposits would be the result of appropriate interest rate pressure.

Under a rigorous monetary base control scheme the authorities would determine the target time path of base money (i.e. bankers' deposits at the Bank of England *plus* notes and coin held by the banks,[4] and would neither supply base money in excess of target amounts* nor absorb surpluses of base money from the banks. The banks would be required to maintain a specified ratio of base money to deposits and would be subject to penalties if the actual ratio deviated significantly from the required ratio in either direction.

It appears at first sight that given this framework official decisions about the amount of base money to be supplied would directly determine the total of bank deposits and thus the stock of money (sterling M3). In fact this is not so. Suppose that the banks' holdings of base money became deficient because the authorities have reduced its supply (or increased it less than expected). In the short run the required ratio of base money to deposits could be restored only by a reduction of both assets and deposits of the banks by an appropriate multiple of the deficiency of base money. It would be necessary to induce deposit holders to use deposits to buy assets supplied by the banks. Thus, interest rates on these assets would need to rise in relation to interest rates paid by the banks on deposits and CDs. Apart from the disadvantages and uncertainties involved – the necessary changes in the structure of rates might not come about (so that the operation would be ineffective); very severe strains might be imposed on banks and financial markets; disintermediation might be induced, etc. – the intended effects that did materialize would have been brought about by the impact of changes in interest rates rather than, directly, by the imposition of restrictions on the supply of base money.[5]

(2) Changes in interest rates occurring as a consequence of the

* The lender of last-resort function of the Bank of England would have to be abolished or, at least, very severely restricted.

authorities' control of the supply of base money might not establish the level and structure of rates needed to keep the growth of the stock of money on its target time path.

A monetary base control system can be devised under which the authorities would supply target amounts of base money by means of open market operations (in the money market) designed either to supplement or to offset (wholly or in part) net cash flows to the banks resulting from government net transactions with the private sector, from the operations of the Exchange Equalization Account, etc. If the banks needed base money in excess of the official target, these excess amounts would be provided by the Bank of England as lender of last resort on penal terms, these terms being more severe for larger excess amounts than for smaller ones. Thus, whenever the total volume of bank deposits increased more than was consistent with the desired growth of the stock of money (sterling M3), the banks would find it necessary to obtain some base money on penal terms.* Consequently, the net acquisition of assets (including the making of new advances) would become less attractive to the banks and would be damped down, resulting in a slowing down of the growth of deposits.

Under such a system, short-term interest rates would rise whenever the banks had recourse to facilities provided by the lender of last resort, and the rise in rates would be greater the larger the amount of base money obtained by the banks in this way. That is to say, changes in interest rates would reflect movements in the banks' demand for base money in relation to its target supply. These changes in interest rates would be generally 'in the right direction', but they might not impose just the degree of pressure necessary to ensure that the stock of money remains on its target path. If the demand for bank loans was strong the banks might choose to incur penal terms imposed by the Bank of England on last-resort loans,[6] so as to acquire base money necessary to support the desired expansion of assets and the corresponding generation of new deposits. Moreover, especially if penal terms levied on last-resort loans fell directly on the banks, movements of other rates might not be such as to induce investors to substitute bills, bonds, etc., for bank deposits. In short, changes in interest rates brought about by official control of the supply of base money might not be those needed to control the rate of monetary growth. Thus, the authorities would need

* It would be necessary to ensure that the banks themselves suffered the penalty, and not the discount houses.

to take action to influence market interest rates, this action being directly related to the growth of the stock of money in relation to its target.

(3) All monetary base control systems would tend to have disadvantageous effects on the structure and operational efficiency of the financial system.

Monetary base control would involve the imposition on banks (and, possibly, finance houses) of penalties in some form if the banking system's actual holdings of, or needs for, base money diverged from the target supply of base money. These penalties – clearly necessary to make the system responsive to official action – would apply to banks but not to other financial institutions. The existence, side by side, of 'controlled' and 'uncontrolled' institutions engaging in very similar business would have several disadvantages. Apart from the problem of equity, competition within the banking sector and between the banks and other financial institutions would be likely to decrease with, probably, significant adverse effects on the allocative efficiency of the system; inducements to innovate and to develop new financial techniques would be blunted; there would be tendencies to disintermediation and re-intermediation.

The authorities attach very considerable importance to these problems, especially disintermediation, though their extent and consequences cannot be estimated *a priori*. But it is the view of the authorities that the likelihood that a new form of control would stimulate substantial disintermediation must be treated as a strong argument against the introduction of such a system or technique of monetary control.

(4) All monetary base control systems would raise a number of difficult operational problems.

In the first place, the authorities would need to determine target amounts of base money to be supplied; the authors of the Green Paper assert that it would be necessary to use daily targets. Clearly, the determination of daily (or even weekly) base money targets would be a matter of extreme difficulty. Daily or weekly base money targets must be derived from estimates of desired stock of sterling M3 (unadjusted) on the relevant dates, these being the amounts of sterling M3 outstanding on those dates considered to be consistent with the published target rate of growth of seasonally adjusted sterling M3 over periods of six months or longer. Monthly data show that unadjusted sterling M3 fluctuates considerably in relation to its longer-term trend and weekly or daily variations are likely to be even more pronounced. Even allowing for the fact that, as the period for which the published monetary target was to be met advanced desired sterling M3 would become easier to estimate, it appears very improbable that daily or weekly base money targets would constitute a reliable and unambiguous basis for monetary control.

Second, there would be considerable difficulties in making the actual amounts of base money supplied (apart, of course, from amounts supplied by the Bank of England as lender of last resort) approximate the target amounts. The problem here is that the type and size of open market operations to be undertaken for this purpose would have to be determined on the basis of forecasts of cash flows to and from the banks. But these cash flows vary considerably from day to day and these variations are often unpredictable. As a result, the banking system could often be forced to acquire more or less base money through last-resort facilities than was intended by the authorities.[7] In such cases changes in interest rates would also be different from the desired changes; moreover, sharp fluctuations in interest rates might occur which would not promote effective control of the stock of money but might impede smooth and efficient operation of financial markets.

Third, under some monetary base control arrangements very difficult forecasting and estimating problems would face the banks. This would be the case if the lead accounting method was used to determine the banks' base money to deposits ratio (the ratio between base money held at time $(t-1)$ and deposits outstanding at time t) so that base money held at time $(t-1)$ set the permitted volume of deposits at a later time t and the banks would suffer penalties if their actual deposits at time t significantly exceeded the permitted level and, perhaps, also if they fall short of that level. Several problems arise in this connection. Bank deposits do not grow steadily: there are considerable short-period fluctuations for the banking system as a whole and even sharper fluctuations in the growth of individual banks' deposits. These fluctuations are largely due to variations in government receipts and payments and to the fact that the timing of the use of overdraft and other loan facilities is usually left to bank customers. The banks cannot foresee these fluctuations accurately, they cannot control them, and the scope for offsetting operations is limited.[8] Thus, if the lead accounting system was adopted the banks' forecasts of their deposits would often be inaccurate. But the authorities would take action according to the observed divergence of the banks' actual holdings of base money from base money targets; i.e., their action would be appropriate only if the banks' forecasts of deposits were in fact correct. If the banks overestimated deposits official action would be too restrictive; if they underestimated them it would allow excessive expansion.

The authors of the Green Paper have presented a strong case against the adoption of a monetary base control system. Their case is somewhat one-sided. In the first place, there is hardly a mention of advantages of such a system. But advantages are clearly possible: for example, it is not unlikely that costs and penalties that the banks would suffer to acquire or hold excessive amounts of base money would induce them to take stronger action to reduce the growth of lending – to raise lending rates not only to pass on increases in the cost of funds but to discourage borrowers, to impose stiffer non-price terms on loans, etc. Second, some of the disadvantages and difficulties discussed in relation to monetary base control schemes are likely to be present, in one form or another, under other arrangements, e.g. problems involved in estimating desired sterling M3 at specific times, and in deciding on measures needed to make actual sterling M3 approximate the desired level. But two fundamental points stand out: (1) the essential instrument of monetary control is the rate of interest and the control can be exercised only by regulating the pressure of the rate of interest on the chosen monetary aggregate (sterling M3); (2) schemes involving penalties falling on banks only induce undesirable disintermediation which tends to reduce the effectiveness of monetary control itself.

The crucial operational importance of changes in interest rates in the control of monetary growth raises the problem of relative advantages of initiating these changes by means of discretionary action of the authorities and by means of changing the rate of interest on last-resort loans automatically, according to a pre-determined scale, whenever a monetary aggregate chosen as an indicator (e.g. sterling M3 or the amount of base money in the hands of the banks) moves off-course. This problem is briefly discussed in the Green Paper under the heading of 'Indicator Systems'.*

* A mechanism specifically mentioned is as follows. The Bank of England would lend to discount houses at the 'operative rate', being the minimum lending rate (determined as at present) *plus* or *minus* an 'adjustment' determined by the deviation of sterling M3 from its target path according to a pre-set graduated scale.

An indicator system has one obvious advantage: changes in interest rates would occur earlier than under the discretionary system. The latter has a built-in bias towards delay because there is a tendency to defer the necessary decision to act until there is a clear case for action. The authorities would have the power to override the automatic mechanism, but to use this power decision-makers would need to make out a case (even if only to themselves) for doing so, that is to say for not causing a change in interest rates. On the other hand, indicator systems have disadvantages. Interest rates would be tied to movements of a single monetary aggregate and the authorities would normally be debarred from using their knowledge, experience, flair, etc., in interpreting other available evidence and from taking decisions on the basis of all relevant considerations. Second, the automatic link established between monetary growth and interest rates would preclude manipulation of the latter for other purposes.

The authors of the Green Paper do not offer a conclusion on the desirability or otherwise of adopting an indicator system. But quite clearly, they show no enthusiasm for this innovation.

Proposals for the reform of the competition and credit control system are set out in the concluding chapter of the Green Paper. They are the logical outcome of the authorities' view that the object of monetary control is the control of monetary growth in the middle term rather than week-by-week or even day-by-day control of the stock of money, and that, given fiscal policy, interest rates must be the main means of monetary control.

(1) The supplementary special deposits scheme is to be discontinued. 'The corset' imposes severe pressures on banks but, because of various processes of disintermediation and, since the abolition of exchange control in November 1979, because of access that UK borrowers have to foreign sources of finance, it is no longer effective in reducing the supply of credit to the private sector. Moreover, disintermediation causes the velocity of circulation to rise, and this means that such restraint of monetary growth as can be ascribed to the operation of the supplementary special deposits scheme is at least partly nullified. Clearly, 'the corset' has lost its usefulness as an instrument of control but it causes a number of distortions and anomalies.

(2) The $12\frac{1}{2}$ per cent minimum reserve ratio is also to be discontinued. Reserve requirements do not constitute an effective mechanical con-

straint on monetary growth. Their purpose in the competition and credit control scheme has been to enable the authorities to engineer changes in short-term interest rates. But as the minimum lending rate is now determined by administrative decision of the Bank of England, the reserve ratio is no longer necessary for this purpose; indeed, its abolition may strengthen the position of the authorities in this respect by enabling them to operate more freely in Treasury bills to reinforce pressures exerted by the manipulation of the minimum lending rate. On the other hand, experience has shown that the imposition of pressure on bank reserves may have perverse effects on interest rates; it tends to stimulate interbank competition for deposits which pushes up interest rates on bank deposits and CDs in relation to rates obtainable on other assets, with the result that the tendency to substitute other assets for deposits is weakened and may be reversed.[9]

(3) The requirement to hold cash (balances with the Bank of England) which under competition and credit control arrangements applies to London clearing banks only is to be extended to all banks. The object of this requirement is to facilitate and make more effective official action to cause changes in interest rates.

If these proposals are put into effect, monetary control will become (given fiscal policy) entirely a matter of manipulation of interest rates. In broad outline the causal sequence implicit in the reform proposals is as follows. An increase in the minimum lending rate, supported by appropriate open market sales of Treasury bills, etc., *causes* a rise in the level and changes in the structure of short-term interest rates (including bank lending rates); these changes in interest rates *cause* adjustments in asset demands and supplies, including substitution of various money market instruments for bank deposits held as assets and, after some time, a fall in the demand for bank advances; the use of bank deposits to buy other assets and a decrease in bank lending (reflecting a fall in the demand for advances) *cause* a reduction in the rate of growth of the total volume of deposits and, therefore, of the stock of money.

The monetary adjustment process just outlined is, obviously, very similar in nature to the competition and credit control adjustment process. Thus, under the proposed regime as under the present arrangements the effects of policy measures on the rate of monetary growth depend on the response of the demand for advances to increases in bank lending rates, on the extent to which changes in interest rates induce deposit holders to use them to buy other assets[10] and on the various offsetting reactions that tend to be generated by changes in financial relationships.

There are reasons to think that if the proposals are implemented the new system will be more effective than the present one. First, the pressure on money market rates will probably be stronger, more sustained[11] and more general.[12] It is, therefore, possible that the pressure that movements of market interest rates exert on bank lending rates will be stronger and that, consequently, the effects on the demand for bank credit will also be stronger. Second, the authorities do not propose to use pressure on bank (cash) reserves as a monetary instrument. In the absence of such pressure the banks will have less incentive to bid for deposits, and so deposit and CD rates will tend to rise less than under the present system. Thus, the diversion of funds from the government to the banks will be reduced and so will government borrowing from the banking sector and the generation of deposits which results from it. Third, it is legitimate to expect that greater generality and evenness in the rise in interest rates, together with the absence of discriminatory pressures on the banks, will reduce the extent of disintermediation. Therefore, at least some of the adjustments that under present arrangements tend to offset reductions in the rate of growth of the stock of money will be eliminated.

Although the proposals in the Green Paper envisage the abolition of the best-known features of the competition and credit control system, they leave intact – indeed, strengthen and accentuate – its most fundamental characteristic: the central role of interest rates in monetary management. Thus, the proposed reform may be looked upon as an important development of the competition and credit control approach to monetary control rather than simply as the abandonment of competition and credit control arrangements.

Notes

CHAPTER 1: *Banks and Financial Markets*

1 This is the classification used since 1975 in banking statistics published in the *Bank of England Quarterly Bulletin.*

2 Since the end of 1975 the Co-operative Bank takes part in the clearing alongside the London clearing banks. But it is not a member of the Committee of London Clearing Bankers and remains listed among other British banks.

3 J. Revell, 'Changes in British Banking – the Growth of the Secondary Banking System', Hill, Samuel Occasional Paper no. 3 (1968); J. Revell, *The British Financial System* (1973).

4 Other deposit banks were of marginal importance except for day-to-day banking business in Northern Ireland which was (and is) in the hands of Northern Ireland banks.

5 But clearing banks had subsidiaries which operated extensively in the fields of secondary banks and in competition with them.

6 The analysis is confined to sterling business of banks because the competition and credit control system (which is the subject matter of the present study) regulates only bank operations in sterling.

7 Banking statistics in the present format are available from May 1975.

8 The proportion tends to be affected by changes in interest rates: when rates rise some funds shift from sight deposits to interest bearing (short) time deposits.

9 A CD is a document issued by a bank certifying that a stated sum has been deposited with it for a stated period at a fixed rate of interest. A CD is a negotiable instrument. About 70% of sterling CDs outstanding are held by banks and discount houses; the issue of CDs thus represents largely funds obtained from other banks.

10 Revell gives £10,000, and in the case of some banks £50,000, as the minimum for sterling deposits and £500,000 as 'probably the norm' for sterling advances. Cf. 'Changes in British Banking', p. 19 and *British Financial System*, pp. 247–8.

11 Japanese banks increased this class of lending (which includes advances to UK registered subsidiaries of Japanese firms) very considerably in the period under review. The relatively high values of the standard deviation reflect growth rather than variability in this case.

12 An extensive literature exists; e.g., W. M. Scammell, *The London Discount Market* (1968); P. Einzig, *Parallel Money Markets*, vol. 1 (1971); Revell, *British Financial System*, chs 8, 10 and 11.

13 £500,000 has often been mentioned as standard in all three cases and £100,000, £10,000 and £25,000 as normal minimum amounts in the interbank, local authority and finance house markets respectively. Cf. Einzig, *Parallel Money Markets*, vol. 1, pp. 47, 110; Revell, *British Financial System*, p. 273.

14 Arrangements are sometimes made directly between lenders and borrowers, especially in the interbank market.

15 If market conditions are very tight the rate on overnight interbank loans tends to rise sharply, sometimes well above rates on three or six-month loans. Banks that had undertaken to make payments must find the necessary money at whatever cost – their search for funds causes the overnight rate to rise sharply. Local authorities and finance houses normally have unused overdraft facilities and do not need to bid for funds. (NB. It is cheaper to borrow at 100% overnight than at 14·5% for seven days.)

16 Eurodollars are dollar balances placed by their owners with banks outside the United States but retaining their dollar denomination and repayable in US dollars. Placements involve transfers of ownership of the dollar balances (deposits with a US bank) from their original owners to banks outside the USA – the 'Eurobanks'. Eurobanks use balances so obtained (1) to make dollar loans to their customers; (2) to place them with other Eurobanks. Operations in Eurodollars are thus of two types: normal banking intermediation, i.e. taking deposits from and making loans to non-bank customers, and interbank dealings. Only the latter are Eurodollar market transactions. These observations apply to other Eurocurrencies, the prefix 'Euro' meaning in effect 'outside the country of origin of the currency in question'; this prefix does not indicate any particular connection with Europe; e.g., a Japanese bank in Tokyo taking sterling deposits is a Eurobank in this context, as is an Indian bank in Bombay taking yen deposits.

17 The international character of Eurocurrency markets presents a difficulty of interpretation of statistics. It is reasonable to postulate that foreign

currency deposits that banks in the UK take from and place with other banks in the UK represent their Eurocurrency market business, whereas deposits from and loans to other UK customers constitute normal banking business in foreign currencies. But foreign currency deposits taken by banks in the UK from, and market loans and advances to, overseas economic units cover both types of business; Eurocurrency market business predominates.

18 This feature of the banking mechanism has given rise to suggestions that the competition and credit control system has not, contrary to the intention of its authors, placed all banks on an equal footing. Cf. E. Victor Morgan and I. M. Richards, 'A Verdict on Competition and Credit Control', *The Banker*, June 1974. See also B. Tew, 'Are Some Banks more Equal than Others?' *The Banker*, October 1974.

19 Needless to say, holdings of other assets are also adjusted.

20 Unless there is a general outflow of reserves from the system, sales of non-reserve assets can be made easily – banks to which reserves have moved are in the market as buyers of non-reserve assets.

21 It should be noted that loans to (deposits with) other banks and acquisitions of other banks' CDs are 'deductibles' in the calculation of eligible liabilities. A bank that lends to another bank thereby reduces its eligible liabilities, other things being the same. Cf. pp. 35–7 for the definition and description of eligible liabilities.

22 Withdrawal of funds from parallel markets is a substitute for other types of asset disposal, e.g. sales of marketable securities. But the value of parallel market assets is capital-certain, whereas security sales may involve capital losses.

CHAPTER 2: *Competition for Deposits*

1 Because deposits with other UK banks and holdings of CDs are 'deductibles'. See below, p. 35.

2 Withdrawals of funds from the local authority and the finance house market cannot be so treated. Although in most cases they cause a shift of funds to banks seeking repayment of loans from banks providing the debtor institutions with means to repay loans, they are clearly operations in assets, usually in the context of rearrangement of assets.

3 The source of data for these charts are UK short-term money rates and UK security yields tables in the *Bank of England Quarterly Bulletin*. Published CD rate and the yield on five-year gilt-edged stocks are comparable only in broad terms; but changes in the relationship between them are large enough to indicate changes in their relative attractiveness to investors.

4 From 1971 until the last quarter of 1974 these institutions' operations in Treasury bills were negligible in amount.

5 If the rate of exchange is fixed the resulting inflow of foreign funds may be very considerable; if the rate is free to fluctuate the inflow of funds is likely to cause an appreciation of sterling spot exchange rate and an increase in the forward discount on sterling (or a decrease in the forward premium), thus reducing the attractiveness of placing foreign funds with UK banks and damping down or stopping the inflow.

6 This happens if in the absence of the inflow the demand for foreign currencies would be greater than their current supply, making the EEA a net seller of foreign currencies for sterling.

7 Cf. W. Greenwell & Co., *Monetary Bulletin*, 17 October 1973, pp. 4–5.

8 Cf. Gordon Richardson, 'Reflections on the Conduct of Monetary Policy', *Bank of England Quarterly Bulletin*, March 1978, p. 32.

9 The outcome is less satisfactory if the same bank lends to a customer and sells a CD to him. Apart from the fact that the CD may carry a higher rate of interest than is charged on the overdraft, an increase in eligible liabilities takes place but there is no accrual of reserves – the bank's reserve position worsens.

10 Loans made to other banks are deductible in the calculation of the lending bank's eligible liabilities.

11 CDs are, of course, marketable; their holders can sell them and use the proceeds to finance outlays. But if they had not bought CDs they would have retained their overdraft facilities and therefore the ability to finance outlays. The ability of the economic units concerned to spend is the same in both cases but holdings of CDs count as 'money' whereas unused overdraft facilities do not.

CHAPTER 3: *The Competition and Credit Control System*

1 Northern Ireland banks have been exempted from the obligation to place special deposits.

2 Except those with eligible liabilities of less than £5 million.

3 This is the ratio of the average amount of these balances held over a banking month to eligible liabilities outstanding on the reporting date of the preceding month.

4 Company tax reserve certificates were originally included in reserve assets but were later phased out.

5 *Bank of England Quarterly Bulletin*, September 1973, pp. 306–7.

6 The terminology was changed: 'specified categories of public sector debt' became known as 'defined assets'.

7 Defined as the three-year moving average of capital and reserves outstanding at the end of December.

8 But the total of special deposits and reserve assets cannot constitute a higher proportion of eligible liabilities of finance houses than of the banks.

9 But the government broker may not be willing to buy stocks with more than one year to final maturity.

10 Northern Ireland banks are, however, free of this obligation.

11 The principal IBELs are: time deposits, the excess of interest bearing deposits (loans) from other banks over interest-bearing placements with other banks, and the excess of issues of CDs over holdings of other banks CDs.

12 The actual level of IBELs in a particular month is defined as the average of the amounts outstanding at the reporting dates in that month and the two preceding months.

13 This schedule was instituted in November 1974; the schedule announced at the introduction of the scheme in December 1973 was more severe: the 5%, 25% and 50% rates applied to excesses of IBEL not greater than 1%, greater than 1% but not greater than 3% and greater than 3% of the base level respectively.

14 See Sir Leslie O'Brien's 'Key Issues in Monetary and Credit Policy', *Bank of England Quarterly Bulletin*, June 1971, pp. 197–8.

15 A detailed discussion of the adjustment process will be presented in chapter 6.

16 Cf. N. Kaldor and J. Trevithick, 'A Keynesian Perspective on Money', *Lloyds Bank Review*, January 1981, pp. 5–7.

CHAPTER 4: *Creation of Reserves within the Banking Sector*

1 As a group financial institutions outside the banking sector hold considerable amounts of these assets, but the banks would need to buy assets from individual institutions, of which there are several hundreds.

2 If the bank in question is a non-clearing bank, the making of new loans depletes its working balance with one of the clearing banks. It then surrenders reserve assets to that clearing bank to rebuild the working balance; this transfer of reserve assets also enables the clearing bank to restore its own reserves, which fell when the non-clearing bank in question drew on its working balance.

3 In the first place Bank A draws on its balance with the Bank of England which it then rebuilds by withdrawing money at call from the discount market. There is no strain on discount houses because as Bank A's balance with the Bank of England falls other banks' balances rise and they increase call loans to discount houses.

4 Some recipients of 'the borrower's' payments are likely to be customers of Bank A, who deposit cheques received from 'the borrower' with Bank A. Instead of surrendering reserve assets in settlement Bank A credits these customers' accounts; i.e., deposits increase. For simplicity this type of adjustment is disregarded in subsequent discussions.

5 Balances with other banks are deductible in calculating eligible liabilities. Bank H does not hold other banks' CDs.

6 Before this has been achieved, expansion by Bank L would be balanced by contraction by Bank K.

7 *Bank of England Quarterly Bulletin*, September 1973, p. 307. The role of this requirement as an instrument of restricting reserve-creating operations was emphasized, as was the importance attached by the Bank to discount houses' compliance with this limit to their total business.

8 *Bank of England Quarterly Bulletin*, Statistical Annex, Table: 'Discount Market'.

9 Ratio of total assets, sterling and foreign currencies, of discount houses and other money market institutions to their aggregate capital and reserves.

10 This is only a rough indication because purchases of all assets, defined as well as undefined, *from private sector holders* channel funds to private sector users and therefore do not cause reserves to flow out of the banking system; on the other hand purchases of defined or undefined assets (e.g., long term gilt edged securities) *from the authorities* cause an outflow of reserves from the banks.

CHAPTER 5: *Public Sector Borrowing from the Banking Sector and its Effect on Bank Reserves*

1 The total currency flow is the sum of: current balance, the net total of investment and other capital flows, and the balancing item.

2 If the total currency flow is positive, the Exchequer must provide sterling funds to enable EEA to make net purchases of foreign currencies.

3 If the total currency flow is positive, borrowing from abroad increases it.

4 Because the total currency flow would be unaffected – inflow of foreign currencies (deposits) would be balanced by their outflow.

5 As the total of bank deposits increases, whether owing to net spending by the public sector or to expansion of bank credit, a fraction of the increase in deposits tends to be withdrawn by bank customers in cash. This reduces the magnitude of the increase during a given period in the banking sector's holdings of public sector debt: either of the banks' holdings of notes and coins or of holdings of Treasury bills by the Banking Department of the Bank of England. The latter takes place if the banks draw notes from the Banking Department and the Banking Department draws newly issued notes from the Issue Department of the Bank of England and passes Treasury bills to it as cover for the increase in the Fiduciary issue. (NB The Issue Department is outside the banking sector.)

6 The excess of purchases of new Treasury bills over maturities of bills held by discount houses.

7 To avoid uncertainties about the timing of Exchequer receipts and

payments it is convenient to treat them as taking place when public deposits are credited or debited.

8 Clearing banks have agreed to maintain balances with the Bank of England amounting, on the average, to $1\frac{1}{2}$% of their eligible liabilities.

9 Having experienced an increase in deposits, the clearing banks retain some additional balances with the Bank of England; the Bank balances this rise in its liabilities by increasing its own holdings of Treasury bills.

10 Treasury bills are supplied from, or absorbed by, the portfolio of the Issue Department of the Bank of England, which lends the proceeds of bill sales to the Exchequer, or finances purchases out of repayment of Ways and Means Advances previously made to the Exchequer. The Issue Department may buy tap Treasury bills instead of making Ways and Means Advances. Market operations in Treasury bills are performed by the Bank of England's agent in the market (the 'special buyer'), Seccombe, Marshall and Campion Ltd – a small discount house.

11 Individual banks may dispose of cash surpluses by making placements in parallel money markets.

12 Discount houses may also find their ability to acquire undefined assets increased (provided that their undefined assets multiple is below its maximum of 20) if and when they succeed in disposing of some of their additional Treasury bills. The practical importance of the increase in this type of banking sector lending to the private sector is unlikely to be substantial.

13 This substitution of non-reserve public sector debt for reserve assets can be accomplished in several ways: e.g., proceeds of maturing Treasury bills may be used by the banks to buy gilt-edged stocks from the government broker; the banks may sell Treasury bills before maturity to the special buyer and use the proceeds to buy gilt-edged stocks (the authorities are very likely to facilitate such transactions); the banks may withdraw money at call from the discount market to finance purchases of stocks – in this case discount houses must sell bills to the special buyer (again, the authorities are likely to co-operate). Some bank purchases of gilt-edged securities from private sector holders can be the instrument of substitution, namely if, and to the extent that, private sector sellers of securities to the banks use the proceeds to buy other gilt-edged securities from the authorities.

14 Special deposits are liabilities of the Bank of England. But the Bank balances special deposits taken from the banks by increasing Banking Department's holdings of government securities (mainly Treasury bills). Thus, special deposits are in effect bank holdings of government debt at one remove.

15 The ratio of currency in circulation to total deposits of the private sector tends to be fairly stable. For example in 1977, apart from seasonal in-

creases in June–July–August and in December, this ratio varied only from 19·7% (in January) to 20·4% (in December), a range of 0·7%.

16 If necessary the banks can restore their balances with the Bank by reducing holdings of other reserve assets.

17 Sources of data: *Bank of England Quarterly Bulletin*, March 1976, March 1977, March 1978, tables 3 and 6/3; March 1979 and December 1979, table 4; *Financial Statistics*, September and November 1979, table 6.5.

18 *Bank of England Quarterly Bulletin* September 1979 (tables 3/1 and 4) records a fall in money at call at £20 million, but if this figure is taken the sum of changes in reserve assets is £22 million, whereas the change in the total is shown as being £23 million. The discrepancy is due to rounding off.

CHAPTER 6: *Control of the Stock of Money*

1 Sir Leslie O'Brien, 'Key Issues in Monetary and Credit Policy', *Bank of England Quarterly Bulletin*, June 1971, p. 197 (reproduced with the Bank's permission).

2 If securities are supplied by the authorities bank deposits are surrendered to them and used to repay public sector debt held by the banks; bank deposits are then extinguished.

3 To the extent that foreign funds are so invested, the inflow of these funds does not enable the banks to sell non-reserve assets.

4 It must also be noted that, to the extent that the decrease in deposits represents placement in financial markets of previously idle balances, this contraction in the stock of money has no effect on the flow of aggregate demand.

5 O'Brien, 'Key Issues', p. 197 (reproduced with the Bank's permission).

6 The difficulties of reducing the supply of bank advances were often discussed in the 1950s and 1960s, when the banks were often 'requested' by the authorities to restrict lending or to reduce the outstanding totals of advances. See for example Sir Oliver Franks, 'The Control of Bank Advances', *Lloyds Bank Review*, January 1961.

7 This important point and the causal sequence that it implies will be further discussed in chapter 9, pp. 131–2.

8 These 'additional' special deposits are payable at each reporting date with respect to eligible liabilities outstanding at the preceding reporting date.

9 It is not inconceivable that special deposits should be required at a rate higher than the banks' desired reserve ratio; but it is inconceivable that a single call for special deposits should specify so high a rate. The present analysis is concerned with effects of a single call.

CHAPTER 7: *Special Deposits*

1 Quantitative information presented in this section is taken (or derived)

from the relevant issues of the *Bank of England Quarterly Bulletin.*

2 If changes in holdings of CDs outside the banking sector are taken as a guide for estimating the spurious element in recorded increases in advances, it appears that expansion of bank credit was genuinely greater in the two months to mid-February 1973 than in the two months to mid-December 1972.

3 During the weeks following tenders on 20 and 27 July, payments for new Treasury bills exceeded repayments by £120 million and £90 million respectively, whereas in the week following the tender on 6 July maturities exceeded new issues by £40 million and in the week following the tender on 13 July maturities balanced new issues.

4 Changes in reserve arrangements for the discount market, which also came into effect on 19 July 1973 (see above p. 39), reduced the discount houses' appetite for Treasury bills and therefore generated another influence pushing Treasury bill rates up.

5 At that time MLR was equal to the average rate of discount on allotment of Treasury bills at the most recent tender *plus* $\frac{1}{2}$% rounded up to the nearest $\frac{1}{4}$%.

6 It must be noted that in the summer and autumn of 1973 arbitrage operations may have caused reported bank lending to overstate expansion; borrowing in anticipation of needs (caused by fears that credit restrictions might be imposed), which also took place, had the same statistical effects. The reported decrease in bank lending to the private sector in the first quarter of 1974 represented, partly, the elimination of these distortions.

7 But the average allotment rate on Treasury bills decreased only a little.

8 On 25 May 1978 the Bank of England announced that the minimum lending rate would thenceforth be determined by administrative decision, in the same way as the Bank rate was fixed before October 1972.

9 The clearing banks were to re-lodge these special deposits when the supplementary special deposits scheme ceased to be operative.

CHAPTER 8: *Supplementary Special Deposits ('the Corset')*

1 Northern Ireland banks are outside the scheme.

2 For this reason some commentators regard it as a substitute for lending ceilings used in the 1950s and 1960s.

3 The percentage yield of the unit, which is the average of yields of assets included in the unit weighted by their proportions in it.

4 A unit of assets should include an appropriate proportion of reserve assets, other liquid assets and interest-bearing special deposits as well as high-yielding loans. For obvious reasons supplementary special deposits displace mainly, or entirely, loans.

5 The weight of supplementary special deposits increases from zero to a figure equal to their rate; the weight of loans decreases by the same amount.

6 Funds now under consideration are most likely to be owned, very largely, by non-bank financial institutions and financially efficient large industrial and commercial companies; they have the knowledge and the facilities to operate in various financial markets.

7 It must be noted that the operations of discount houses are subject to the rule that a house's holdings of undefined assets must not exceed 20 times its capital and reserves and also to the general requirement that the relationship between a house's capital and reserves and the total volume of borrowed funds must be 'appropriate'.

8 Acceptances are not IBELs; they yield commission to the banks and, since bills accepted by banks can be discounted easily and cheaply, make commercial bills good substitutes for short-term bank loans.

9 In the case of a non-clearing bank, repayment of an interbank deposit involves a drawing on that bank's working balance with a clearing bank. Reserve assets of the repaying bank decrease, when (or if) it decides to replenish its working balance.

10 A fall in rates on deposits at seven days' notice reduces their attractiveness relatively to current accounts; if the rate reduction is substantial a shift of balances from deposit to current accounts can be expected to take place, i.e. IBELs will fall. But this shift of balances is likely to be a very slow process, too slow to be significant in the adjustment of the banks' IBELs positions.

11 Quantitative information presented in this section is taken (or derived) from the relevant issues of the *Bank of England Quarterly Bulletin*.

12 These are annual rates computed from actual rates recorded in the periods in question, i.e. percentage annual increases which would have taken place if the recorded rates of growth had been maintained for a year.

13 The decrease in the rate shown for December 1973–June 1974 reflects large repayment of government debt to the banking sector during that period.

14 In their written evidence to the Wilson Committee, published under the title *The London Clearing Banks* (1978), p. 72.

15 The rate of utilization of overdrafts decreased over that period; e.g., *London Clearing Banks*, p. 89. After the revival of the demand for credit in the second quarter of 1977 the Bank of England described it as 'moderate'; cf. *Bank of England Quarterly Bulletin*, September 1977, p. 296.

16 The behaviour of advances is a good indication of the course of total bank lending to the private sector. By accepting customers' bills the banks enable customers to obtain funds from non-bank sources.

17 The banks must provide discount houses with funds to finance purchases of bills. This can easily be done by means of two (linked) transactions: (1) the banks redeem maturing CDs held by the houses or buy CDs from them and reduce call money lent to the discount market; (2) the banks make new call loans to discount houses as the latter make payments for bills. As a result of these operations the banks' net issues of CDs decrease (IBELs fall) and new deposits resulting from the discount houses' bill purchases are at least partly current account deposits (NIBELs). Reserves of the banking system are unaffected. Discount houses replace CDs by commercial bills (both undefined assets).

18 The formula linking MLR to the average rate on allotment of Treasury bills was abandoned in May 1978 and the old 'Bank Rate' method of fixing MLR by administrative decision of the Bank of England was re-introduced.

CHAPTER 9: *Competition and Credit Control – on Appraisal*

1 Cf. W. T. C. King, 'Should Liquidity Ratios be Prescribed?' *The Banker*, April 1956, pp. 189–90. It is true that open market operations directly affect the volume of deposits; but if the market is initially in equilibrium additional purchases of securities from or their sales to the authorities must be induced by changes in security prices – in other words, changes in the volume of bank deposits are brought about by changes in interest rates.

2 i.e. a change in the rate of growth of the stock of money (M3 or sterling M3).

3 Sir Leslie (now Lord) O'Brien, 'Key Issues in Monetary and Credit Policy', *Bank of England Quarterly Bulletin*, June 1971, p. 197 (reproduced with the Bank's permission).

4 Total spending by the private sector accounts for a large proportion of aggregate demand. It must be noted that decreases in spending, which constitute the direct counterpart of a fall in the demand for bank credit, reduce receipts of other economic units and thus force them to reduce their outlays.

5 In the case of open market operations undertaken to reduce the stock of money, economic units surrender bank deposits to the authorities; the authorities exercise these claims on the banks; deposits are then cancelled and the banks surrender an equal amount of reserve assets to the authorities.

6 Assuming that the original level of transactions balances was not excessive.

7 Cf. C. A. E. Goodhart and A. D. Crockett, 'The Importance of Money', Appendix II, *Bank of England Quarterly Bulletin*, June 1970.

8 It must be borne in mind that in the 'normal' range of interest rates a rise by

one percentage point represents a large proportional rise in the rate of interest; e.g., an increase from 10% to 11% is a rise by 10%.

9 The range of permitted short-period variations in the rate of growth of M3 (annualized) would, of course, need to be wider than the target range for the year as a whole.

10 Cf. M. D. K. W. Foot, C. E. A. Goodhart and A. C. Hotson, 'Monetary Base Control', *Bank of England Quarterly Bulletin*, June 1979.

11 By changing the minimum lending rate (formerly Bank rate), by altering the terms of last resort loans to the discount market, by manipulating the issue of Treasury bills, and by market operations in Treasury and other bills, etc.

12 See, e.g., B. Griffiths, 'How the Bank has Mismanaged Monetary Policy', *The Banker*, December 1976.

13 R. S. Sayers, *Central Banking after Bagehot* (1957), p. 107.

14 It should be noted that one of the principal criticisms of the pre-1971 system of lending ceilings was that it blunted competitive incentives, prevented innovation and that, consequently, it caused inefficiency in banking.

15 By reducing non-bank lending to the government and thus forcing it to increase borrowing from the banking sector.

16 National Giro became a listed bank (National Girobank) in October 1978.

17 But non-clearing banks hold non-interest-bearing working balances (deposits) with the clearing banks.

18 It must be noted, however, that there are other costs of operating the payments mechanism.

19 They are 'deductibles' in the calculation of the holding bank's eligible liabilities.

20 Other things being the same, additions to working balances with other banks reduce eligible liabilities.

21 Unless the operations were undertaken to use excess working balances, in which case the clearers would have had an inflow of reserves as excess balances accumulated.

22 This is the case of open market sales undertaken by the authorities to reduce reserves and eligible liabilities of the banks.

23 It is intended to bring Trustee Savings Banks into the scheme in due course.

24 Keen competition between banks and building societies for deposits can cause a sharp rise in interest rates on both deposits and loans. To limit this rise interest rates on bank deposits of less than £10,000 were restricted between September 1973 and February 1975.

25 Special rules and arrangements would be necessary because the nature of business of these institutions is very different from that of the banking business.

26 Except that Northern Ireland banks have not been called upon to place special deposits.

Postscript

1 Fiscal policy also influences monetary growth independently of PSBR; e.g., some fiscal measures may affect private sector demand for bank credit.

2 See 'The Gilt Edged Market', *Bank of England Quarterly Bulletin*, June 1979, for a discussion of possible changes in characteristics of gilt-edged instruments and in marketing techniques which may make the demand for gilt-edged securities steadier than it has been in recent years.

3 For example, if banks are prevented from making new loans the growth of the stock of money is damped down. But if, instead of lending, the banks accept their customers' bills, which other financial institutions buy while selling CDs to the banks (bills accepted by banks are virtually perfect substitutes for CDs), lending by other financial institutions increases because previously idle deposits are used to finance it.

4 Other definitions are possible.

5 This was noted by M. Stewart; cf. 'When Rules and Regulations Do Not Help', *The Times*, 12 May 1980.

6 These additional costs of loanable resources would be passed on to borrowers in higher interest charges.

7 This problem could be avoided by requiring the banks to hold for reserve purposes specially designed instruments purchasable from the Bank of England. The supply of 'base money' would then be independent of cash flows. Such a scheme is mentioned in the Green Paper under the heading of 'Negotiable Entitlements'.

8 This raises the problem of fairness of penalizing the banks if their forecasts are inaccurate.

9 The proposed abolition of the mandatory minimum reserve ratio does not imply that the authorities attach little importance to the liquidity position of the banks. On the contrary: a separate consultative document issued by the Bank of England – 'The Measurement of Liquidity' – sets out proposed liquidity arrangements and requirements much more elaborate than the pre-1971 liquid assets ratio of not less than 28%. Liquidity requirements are proposed for prudential reasons but, since excess holdings of liquid assets provide a basis for expansion leading to an acceleration of monetary growth, the authorities propose to retain the power to call for special deposits to reduce excess liquidity of the banking system if necessary.

10 Deposits so used are likely to be, at least partly, *idle* money balances.

11 Open market operations force discount houses to borrow from the Bank of England on penal terms; to repay these debts the houses sell assets and surrender bank deposits so acquired to the Bank of England. The banks therefore lose cash, and in order to recover it withdraw call money from the discount market compelling the discount houses to borrow again from the Bank of England. Thus, the houses continue to sell assets or to bid for loans and these operations make interest rates rise and keep them up.

12 Under present arrangements the banks bid strongly for Treasury bills and other eligible reserve assets, damping down increases in yields of these assets. If the proposed changes are put into effect demand for the present eligible reserve assets is likely to be less strong relatively to demand for other liquid assets.

Select Bibliography

Artis, M. J., 'Monetary Policy in the 1970s in the Light of Recent Developments', *in* H. G. Johnson and A. R. Nobey (eds), *Issues in Monetary Economics* (1974).

Artis, M. J. and Meadows, P., 'Special Deposits: Old and New', *The Banker*, May 1974.

Bain, A. D., *Control of Money Supply*, 2nd edn (1976).

Bank of England (articles on competition and credit control from the *Bank of England Quarterly Bulletin*, 1971–78):

'Competition and Credit Control', June 1971.

'Key Issues in Monetary and Credit Policy – an Address by the Governor', June 1971.

'Competition and Credit Control: the Discount Market', September 1971.

'Reserve Ratios and Special Deposits', September 1971, supplement.

'Competition and Credit Control' – an Extract from a Lecture by the Chief Cashier, December 1971.

'Reserve Ratios: Further Definitions', December 1971.

'Competition and Credit Control: Further Developments', March 1973.

'Competition and Credit Control: Modified Arrangements for the Discount Market', September 1973.

'Credit Control: A Supplementary Scheme', March 1974.

'Reflections on the Conduct of Monetary Policy' – a Lecture by the Governor, March 1978.

'The Supplementary Scheme: A Summary of Developments from 1974 to 1978'.

Bank of England and the Treasury, *Monetary Control*, Cmnd 7858, London, HMSO, 1980.

Banker, The, 'Symposium on New Credit Controls', *The Banker*, October 1971.

Coghlan, R. T., 'A Transactions Demand for Money', *Bank of England Quarterly Bulletin*, March 1978.

—— 'A New View of Money', *Lloyds Bank Review*, July 1978.

Committee of London Clearing Bankers, *The London Clearing Banks* (1978).

Cramp, A. B., 'The Bank of England Proposals – Implications for Monetary Policy', *Bankers' Magazine*, July 1971.

Courakis, A. S., 'Monetary Policy, Old Wisdom Behind a New Façade', *Economica*, February 1973.

Davis, E. W. and Yeomans, K. A., 'Competition and Credit Control: The Rubicon and Beyond', *Lloyds Bank Review*, January 1973.

Donaldson, W. B., 'Competition and Credit Control – A Commercial Banker's View' (Ernest Sykes Memorial Lecture 1971), *Journal of the Institute of Bankers*, December 1971.

Duck, N. W. and Sheppard, D. K., 'A Proposal for the Control of the U.K. Money Supply', *Economic Journal*, March 1978.

Foot, M. D. K. W., Goodhart, C. A. E. and Hotson, A. C., 'Monetary Base Control', *Bank of England Quarterly Bulletin*, June 1979.

Gowland, D., *Monetary Policy and Credit Control* (1978).

Griffiths, B., 'How the Bank has Mismanaged Monetary Policy', *The Banker*, December 1976.

Harrington, R. L., 'The Importance of Competition for Credit Control', *in* H. G. Johnson and A. R. Nobey (eds), *Issues in Monetary Economics* (1974).

Johnson, H. G., 'Problems of Efficiency in Monetary Management', *Journal of Political Economy*, September/October 1968.

Kern, D., 'Monetary Aspects of the Current Economic Debate', *National Westminster Bank Review*, August 1975.

Lomax, D. F., 'Reserve Assets and Competition and Credit Control', *National Westminster Bank Review*, August 1973.

—— 'Efficiency, Competition and Credit Control', *in* H. G. Johnson and A. R. Nobey (eds), *Issues in Monetary Economics* (1974).

—— 'The Role of Monetary Policy Today', *National Westminster Bank Review*, February 1977.

—— 'Monetary Policy', *National Westminster Bank Review*, August 1978.

Marks, P., 'Competition and Credit Control – The First Eighteen Months', *The Banker*, March 1973.

Midland Bank Review, 'The Supplementary Credit Control Scheme', *Midland Bank Review*, August 1974.

Midland Bank Review, 'Sterling, the Supply of Money and Interest Rates: an Exposition', *Midland Bank Review*, Autumn 1977.

—— 'The Banking Sector and Monetary Policy', *Midland Bank Review*, Winter 1978.

—— 'Monetary Policy and Regulations Imposed on Listed Banks', *Midland Bank Review*, Summer 1979.

Morgan, E. V. and Harrington, R. L., 'Reserve Assets and the Supply of Money', *Manchester School*, March 1973.

—— and Richards, I. M., 'A Verdict on Competition and Credit Control', *The Banker*, June 1974.

Morrison, I. and Brown, R., 'Monetary and Credit Controls in the United Kingdom', *The Banker*, August and September 1975.

O'Brien, Sir L., 'Key Issues in Monetary and Credit Policy' (Address to the International Banking Conference, Munich, May 1971), *Bank of England Quarterly Bulletin*, June 1971.

Page, J. B., 'Competition and Credit Control: The New Approach' (Ernest Sykes Memorial Lecture), *Journal of the Institute of Bankers*, December 1971.

Parkin, M., 'The Discount Houses' Role in the Money Supply Control Process under the "Competition and Credit Control" Regime', *Manchester School*, March 1973.

Posner, M. (ed.), *Demand Management* (1978).

Revell, J., *The British Financial System* (1973).

Richardson, Sir G., 'Reflections on the Conduct of Monetary Policy' (Mais Lecture), *Bank of England Quarterly Bulletin*, March 1978.

Shaw, E. R., *The London Money Market* (1975).

Tew, B., 'Are some Banks more Equal than Others?' *The Banker*, October 1974.

Tsiang, S. C., 'The Diffusion of Reserves and the Money Supply Multiplier', *Economic Journal*, June 1978.

Wood, G. E., 'Cash Base Control of Money Supply', *The Banker*, July 1979.

Index